THE ART OF MATCHING CHARTS

The Art of Matching Charts

Gayatri Devi Vasudev

MOTILAL BANARSIDASS PUBLISHERS
PRIVATE LIMITED • DELHI

Reprint: Delhi, 2008
Second Revised and Enlarged Edition: 2002, 2004
First Edition: 2001

ISBN: 978-81-208-1847-7 (Cloth)
ISBN: 978-81-208-1769-2 (Paper)

MOTILAL BANARSIDASS
41 U.A. Bungalow Road, Jawahar Nagar, Delhi 110 007
8 Mahalaxmi Chamber, 22 Bhulabhai Desai Road, Mumbai 400 026
236, 9th Main III Block, Jayanagar, Bangalore 560 011
203 Royapettah High Road, Mylapore, Chennai 600 004
Sanas Plaza, 1302 Baji Rao Road, Pune 411 002
8 Camac Street, Kolkata 700 017
Ashok Rajpath, Patna 800 004
Chowk, Varanasi 221 001

Printed in India
BY JAINENDRA PRAKASH JAIN AT SHRI JAINENDRA PRESS,
A-45 NARAINA, PHASE-I, NEW DELHI 110 028
AND PUBLISHED BY NARENDRA PRAKASH JAIN FOR
MOTILAL BANARSIDASS PUBLISHERS PRIVATE LIMITED,
BUNGALOW ROAD, DELHI 110 007

Dedicated to my beloved parents
Dr. B.V. Raman and Mrs. Rajeswari Raman
who have made me what I am today.

Preface

Interest in astrology today has assumed a never-before kind of dimension. This has been due to the one-man crusade of Dr. B.V. Raman for over 6 decades to impress on the educated public the scientific foundations of astrology and the tremendous potential it carries in addressing the various ills of society.

The fundamental unit of society is the family. This unit faces great danger today and is more or less in a state of disintegration with more broken families everywhere than ever before. The reason for this sad state of affairs is not difficult to gauge and can be traced to the increasing fragility of marriages all around the globe. Divorce, separation and single parenting have combined to produce children with deep psychological scars that make them quite unfit to face the emotional challenges involved in their own adult lives, especially in man-woman relationships. It is only in India, inspite of various cultural and other onslaughts on her social fabric, that the institution of marriage and therefore, the building block of society, the family, continues to be in relatively good shape. This can be attributed to the high percentage of stable marriages in Indian society where a marriage, even today, is finalized, in most cultured families, on the basis of horoscopes. In other words, the role of horoscope matching in contributing to the health of the marriage, and therefore, of Indian society, is indisputable.

Matching of charts for marriage is not an easy job. It requires many years of practical experience as well as a good understanding of the theoretical aspects of astrology. Many a time, horoscope matching is entrusted to the family priest or a friend who, on the basis of the Kuta agreement *(Porutham)* found in almost every panchanga (traditional almanac), either endorses or rejects the match outright. Such a snap-shot approach to the intricacies of horoscope matching, many times, leads to disastrous results and brings a bad name to astrology.

In the nearly thirty years I spent working in astrology under DR. B.V. RAMAN, I was able to watch the great circumspection with which he approached the task of horoscope matching. He was never a professional astrologer but many friends would come to him for guidance. He seldom paid importance to Kuta agreement. He generally approved or rejected the match over the general strengths of the charts than merely on the Janma Rasis or Janma Nakshatras to which horoscope matching has been reduced to by half-baked practitioners of astrology. Such a slipshod and indifferent approach to matching has several times led to grave marital tragedies where either one of the spouses has died prematurely or irreconcilable differences have erupted between the couple damaging the union beyond repair. When this happens, the blame is conveniently shifted to the marriage Muhurtha or the horoscopes being wrongly cast, both reasons being absolutely untenable to a conscientious student of astrology.

One of the first steps in predictive astrology and which includes matching, and which DR. RAMAN always emphasized strongly as absolutely necessary, is to check the correctness of the charts of the boy and the girl furnished by the parties. Only after ensuring this, can we proceed to the next step of analysing the chart. Therefore, anyone who puts the blame for wrong matching on wrong charts may be deemed to be ill-qualified to do the responsible job of comparison. Of course, now, with computers casting the horoscope, the excuse of wrong charts cannot work any more.

Muhurtha is a time-point defined by well-laid principles of astrology and planetary positions such that any activity initiated at that moment of time has a harmonious take-off. But a Muhurtha, no matter how good, cannot replace the indications in the birth chart. It can, at best, enhance the existing favourable natal indications or in their absence, dilute the malefic significance of a natal chart. In other words, shifting the blame on Muhurtha for a marital mishap resulting from a badly done job of matching is like putting the cart before the horse.

In cases of marital disasters occurring inspite of matching charts (invariably done by those ill-equipped to do it), I found the reasons for the mishap were inherent in the charts themselves and had been simply overlooked and not handled at all, possibly because it was thought Kuta agreement was the entire process of matching. The longevity would be poor or the indications for marital misery would be very strong or multiple unions would be shown by the natal planetary positions. Such situations needed corrective planetary factors from the other chart. Where this had been done, probably by some experienced well-versed astrological savant, I found the marriages survived and this, despite major planetary afflictions. It was then I realised how important it was to take a very careful and deep look at each of the charts from different angles before venturing an opinion. In some cases, the afflictions can be so bad and so severe, nothing can be done about them and the only solution then is stoical acceptance of what awaits the native. This happens in the medical world too where the best expertise and the most sophisticated techniques simply fail to help in certain cases. However, as in medicine, in astrology too, the majority of cases can benefit from a judicious use of the principles of horoscope matching.

Marriages sometimes end in dowry-related tragedies. This led me to pay particular attention to horoscopic features that indicate such unhappy developments and which I have dealt with in a separate chapter. A careful study of the chart, while matching, can alert parents to dowry dangers before it is too late.

Likewise, astrological indications for early widowhood need not cause panic. There are methods to diffuse such indications at the time of matching. Early detection of such horoscopic features can even help in planning not only the young girl's marriage but also her future life by impressing upon the parents, the need to pay equal, if not greater, attention to her education and career. A separate chapter covers the topic of widowhood.

I also found that unusually but also unerringly, the Sun also has a strong adverse impact on marital life when placed in certain sensitive zones of a chart. While Mars, Saturn, Rahu and Ketu are universally acknowledged as malefic and, under certain conditions, as leading to marital havoc, the Sun's role in causing such adversity is, by and large, never recognised. After a careful study of innumerable charts, I found the Sun could be no less responsible for such unhappiness and more especially, in his Dasa, and which I have discussed in the following pages.

Marriages are sometimes finalized without matching of charts. This is because of the wide ignorance amongst parents of the importance of matching of charts and of its role in staving off post-marital dangers. Sometimes, matching is overlooked due to a strong prejudice against astrology. Both situations can be remedied by an open mind and diligent study of the subject. The sole reason for scoffing at astrology is because it has no official recognition and is not part of the academic curriculum, whether at school or college level, which also explains the many misconceptions concerning both its scope and limitations.

DR. RAMAN's one desire in life was to bring astrology into the portals of the university so that this ancient heritage of our land could be applied to improve the quality of life at all levels. Unfortunately, for reasons best known only to those entrusted with our educational system, astrology has been denied a place in it. Of course, we are the losers for it. However, with more and more educated people, and more especially, brilliant Indians with excellent academic backgrounds evincing great interest in various aspects of astrology, it may not be long before DR. RAMAN's efforts will be recognised in the West when Jyotisha will be given its due place in the academia in our own country too. This has always been the pattern with Indian brilliance and attainments. Formal recognition must come from the West first, then only will it follow in our land. Astrology is already causing ripples in thinking circles in the West.

This volume on the important subject of horoscope matching is meant to give a correct idea of the complex process involved in it. This book is a compilation of my editorials that have appeared earlier in THE ASTROLOGICAL MAGAZINE. The illustrations and the questions and answers are additional and aimed at clearing some common doubts usually encountered while matching charts. I am sure the book will help in removing many misconceptions on the subject amongst the laymen and in educating the students on the complex art of matching.

I express my thanks to my brother Mr. Niranjan Babu for his suggestions during the typesetting process.

I also thank Mr. K. Gopinath for typing the manuscript neatly, Mr. Y. Sanjeeva Rao for his suggestions, assistance and meticulous care in reading the proofs and Mr. Manohar, for the well-done job of typesetting.

I also express my sincere appreciation to Mr. J.P. Jain of Motilal Banarsidass Publishers Pvt. Ltd., for his interest in publishing this volume and his continuing support to our crusade for astrology.

June 30, 2000 **Gayatri Devi Vasudev**
Bangalore

Contents

Chapter I

The First Steps

I

Matching of charts for marriage is a very important area of astrology. Matching becomes indispensable if we realise that there are more factors than meet the eye that go to make a marriage not only happy but also lasting.

Matching is, as often wrongly understood, not the first stage of negotiating an alliance. It is reserved until all other considerations have been taken into account.

When a prospective groom or bride is found unsuitable at the very first instance, there is no point in commending the match on astrological grounds. For example, such unsuitability may arise out of a wide difference in academic qualification, physical appearance, cultural or economic backgrounds in which case there would be no point in studying the charts since common sense would warn against such a match. Sooner or later, in most cases, such differences surface bringing in an ever-widening gap between the two, making marital life meaningless.

The task of matching begins only after the boy and girl have been found suitable in factors which can be gleaned through the diligent use of our faculties of the intellect and the senses.

There are 4 factors, each of varying importance, that must be considered thoroughly before coming to a conclusion. The much touted practice of Kuta agreement does not deserve the importance it is usually given nor is it to be a decisive factor in matching.

The 4 factors are :

(1) Longevity

(2) Mental and psychological health

(3) Factors showing more than one marriage

(4) Malefic content or Dosha

Kuta agreement comes only after these four factors have been found satisfactory.

An approximate estimate of longevity of either party to the match is indispensable. Premature death of either party to the match could result in great pain and unhappiness and therfore, charts with too short a life-span, whatever their other merits, must be rejected.

The importance of longevity is highlighted in the following case. The relevant parts of a letter dated 8-4-1993 are reproduced here :

I am furnishing hereunder the birth details and the horoscope of a young girl which were given to me by a friend in the first week of March 1993 for matching with another chart for marital compatibility. I told my friend that the two horoscopes matched well and he could go ahead with the alliance.

A tragic event took place thereafter. The girl died on 12-3-1993 in the bomb-blast in the Air India Building at Nariman Point, Bombay. She was working in the Bank of Oman which was situated on the ground floor of the Air India Building.

When the horoscope was given to me for matching, a week before the event, I could not foresee the tragedy.

Yet another reader wrote to us on 4-5-1993 :

I have been referred to you by X from Calcutta. I had been looking for a suitable alliance since 1987 for my only daughter whose horoscope is enclosed herewith.

I was not successful in getting a proper alliance for her till 13-3-1993. She was employed in the Bank of Oman Ltd., Bombay, which was housed in the Air India Building, Nariman Point.

There was a bomb-blast in the building on the afternoon of 12-3-1993 (Friday) at about 2-45 p.m. A bomb placed in a car in the parking lot of the building blew up the walls and the false ceiling and everything came down. My daughter was hit by a big piece of mortar and she fell unconscious. She was rushed to the Bombay Hospital by the bank staff. She underwent head surgery on the night of 12-3-1993 but her condition deteriorated and she passed away on the morning of 13-3-1993 at around 10-30 a.m. Many days have passed since then but our minds are numb. Why did she die while so many others escaped death ?

In the first case, though the chart had been cleared for marital matching, the reader had not foreseen her premature and tragic death.

Perhaps, the Nakshatras in the two charts were found to be in agreement and so they had been okayed. Yet, how was it the girl died ?

Such cases highlight the importance of matching

charts for marriage with great care and in even greater detail.

One of the foremost tasks incumbent on the matching job is to first assess the longevity of the individuals concerned. It is not necessary the exact span of life and the possible date and month of death should be determined. What is needed is to examine the charts for premature death or short life. Where the approximate longevity estimates of the two charts show a wide gap, then matching becomes redundant. Where one chart shows short life and the other, a long life, the compatibility tests need not be carried out and the pair must be declared as not suitable. Certain delicacies are involved when communicating such information to the young people or their parents seeking the compatibility report. The aim of astrology is to ensure the welfare of all concerned and this must always be borne in mind when expressing an astrological opinion. **At such times, though we are not bound to give the specific detail of Alpayus or short life, we have a duty to express an opinion against the match in strong terms.**

In the first case, before concluding on the compatibility, the longevity should have been estimated approximately.

The span of life is divided into 4 categories :

1) Balarishta
2) Alpayu
3) Madhyayu
4) Purnayu

Balarishta covers cases of infant mortality and childhood deaths. The range is from 0 to 8 years.

Alpayu is reckoned from 8 to 32 years and is understood to imply short life, but not death in infancy or childhood.

If the life-span is somewhere between 33 and 75 years, it is described as Madhyayu.

The last category comprises of cases with a longevity stretching beyond 75 years or Purnayu.

There are standard combinations given in most classical works for these different categories of Ayus or longevity.

We shall not go into the specific combinations for all these categories except to concentrate on those for Alpayu as this becomes a most important factor in rejecting a chart at the very first step of the matching process. Even in considering combinations for Alpayu, since marital negotiations are to be initiated only after 18 years (for girls) and 23 years for boys according to statutory law as well contemporary social custom, combinations that do not support longevity after 18 years become important.

(a) If the Lagna lord is exalted but not aspected by any benefic planet and Saturn occupies Sagittarius or Pisces Navamsa, the term of life is 19 years.

(b) When the Moon occupies the 6th or the 8th from Lagna and malefic planets in Kendras do not receive any benefic aspects death comes in the 20th year.

(c) If Mars and Jupiter are in Lagna and the Moon is in the 7th while the 8th house is occupied by a planet — benefic or malefic — the life-span is 22 years.

(d) If Lagna lord is in Lagna, the 8th lord is in the 9th

and the planet in the 8th is aspected by a malefic—24 years.

(e) If the 8th and 12th lords are devoid of strength and Saturn occupies Lagna in a common sign, death occurs at 25 years.

(f) If Mars is in Lagna and the Sun and Saturn occupy quadrants, life ends at 20 years.

(g) If the 8th lord from Lagna or the Moon be in the 12th or a Kendra — the native lives for 28 years.

(h) If Saturn occupies the Lagna in an inimical sign and benefics are in the 3rd, 6th, 9th or 12th — 26 or 27 years.

(i) When the Sun, the Moon and Saturn conjoin in the 8th house, the native lives for 29 years.

(j) When the 8th lord is in a Kendra and the Lagna lord is weak, the native lives for 32 years.

(k) If Mercury in strength occupies a Kendra and the 8th house be free of occupation by any planet, the native dies in his 30th year.

(l) If the Lagna lord and the Moon be weak and occupy Apoklimas (the 3rd, the 6th, the 9th, the 12th) and be aspected by malefics, the native lives for 32 years.

(m) If the Lagna be occupied by the Sun and be hemmed on either side by malefics, the native lives upto 31 years.

(n) When there are no benefics in Kendras and the 8th house is occupied by a planet, the native lives for 30 years.

(o) When the 8th lord being Saturn or a malefic in

conjunction with another malefic planet occupies an evil Shashtyamsa, it shows short life.

(p) When the Lagna is occupied by malefics and the Moon also is with malefics with no benefic aspects, Alpayu results.

In all these cases, the exact span of life indicated against each combination may or may not turn out to be accurate. But, the important point to be noted is that, in a broad sense, a short life is indicated. It may be any time before 32 years. Sometimes, some mild exonerating factor may stretch Ayus to slightly beyond this.

For example, a chart that may survive the 32nd year may succumb to a Maraka factor when 35 or 38 or even 39 years when also, the chart could be brought under the short-life category.

Combinations for Balarishta, especially those that have the Moon in the Dustanas, the 6th, 8th or the 12th — and afflicted by Rahu or Mars or Saturn alone or in

Chart 1 : Female : Born 15-12-1964 at 16h. 4m. (IST) at 18 N 58, 72 E 50 with a balance of 1 year, 2 months and 2 days of Ketu Dasa at birth.

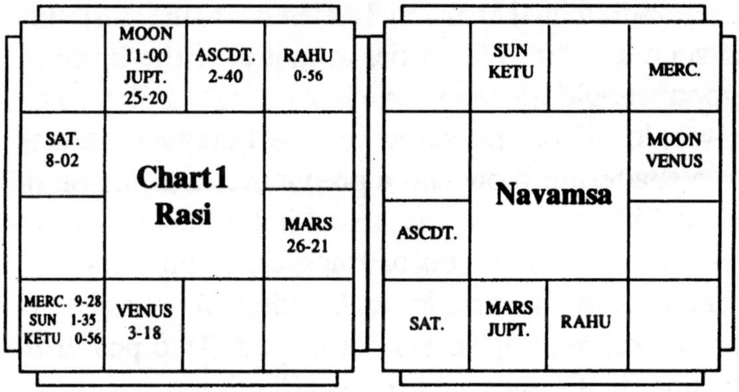

combination can also make one vulnerable to early death.

In the Bombay-blast cases, where the **longevity point** was missed by the reader when approving the chart for marriage, we find Taurus rising aspected by the Ascendant lord Venus in Chart 1. Malefics — natural — Mars and Saturn occupy the two Kendras, the 4th and the 10th powerfully. The Moon is in the 12th with Jupiter. Jupiter, in turn, is the 8th lord (Ayustanadhipati) and his being relegated to the 12th tends to decimate Ayus. Combination (g) requiring the 8th lord from Lagna or the Moon being in the 12th or Kendra is fulfilled with 8th lord Jupiter *plus* the Moon occupying the 12th. The native died in her 28th year. The exact combination and the text-book result tally. But this is rare and infrequent. What we should bear in mind is that, it is not material to know if death will come at 28 years. What is really of importance to us is, the chart shows short life and it should not matter if death should occur in her 24th year, 28th year or 30th year or even the 31st. The different life-spans do not make a substantial or material difference to the feasibility of such a chart. What does it matter if the bride or groom should die when one is 28 or when 33 years ? It would all be the same for the bereaved spouse — a shattering blow and a premature termination of marital life which is what matching of charts tries to avoid or overcome using astrological parameters.

Apart from the specific combination, Venus as Lagna lord aspecting Lagna has not helped. Two powerful malefics in Kendras are a heavy affliction.

Venus, though in a Kendra, occupies Visakha, a Nakshatra ruled by 8th lord Jupiter who himself is pushed to the 12th.

Chart 2 : Female : Born 13-12-1964 at 00-07 a.m. (IST) at 18 N 58, 72 E 50 with a balance of 2 years, 8 months and 29 days of Mars Dasa at birth.

	JUPT(R) 29-13		RAHU 2-40
SAT. 6-32 MOON 1-26	Chart 2 Rasi		ASCDT. 25-11
			MARS 11-32
KETU 2-40	MERC. 14-29	SUN 28-30	VENUS 23-05

	KETU		SUN
ASCDT.	Navamsa		MARS VENUS
JUPT.	SAT. MERC.	RAHU MOON	

In the second case (Chart 2), the Lagna lord Moon is in the 8th, the worst Dustana, afflicted by the 8th lord Saturn as well as malefic Mars. The Lagna is hemmed between malefics, Rahu and Mars. The heavy affliction to the Ascendant tends to weaken the Ascendant or the well-being of the body.

Both charts have the combined influence of Mars-Saturn on the Ascendant lord. Chart 1 has Mars-Saturn aspecting the Lagna lord Venus. Chart 2 has Mars and Saturn aspecting the Lagna lord Moon in the 8th.

In considering the Ayus of any chart, the Moon afflicted in the 8th by the malefics Sun, Moon, Saturn or Rahu is always to be interpreted cautiously and can show sudden and premature death.

Assessment of longevity, even if done approximately, is quite a tough job. Classical works carry many methods for doing it and some of these give fairly good results. Some of the methods lead to conclusions that go wide off the mark. They have to be carefully applied and judiciously interpreted before coming to a conclusion on the life-span of the individuals concerned.

In the case of young man, who was a brilliant student of astrology, an astrological assessment of his own chart prevented him from letting his mother pursue any marital alliances. In our country, even today, hundreds of academically qualified and vocationally well-placed boys and girls leave it to their parents to choose their marital partner for them. This, the parents take upon themselves as a moral and filial duty and carefully screen many proposals before finalising one. The family background ranks high in the list of important factors followed only next by the appearance and qualification of the potential bride or groom. These factors, even if found satisfactory, are not final. The horoscopes must match. Otherwise, no matter how eligible in terms of family, looks, academic degrees, affluence etc., the match is seldom approved. Such careful and methodical selection of marital partners makes the institution of marriage in India a solid and sustaining unit of society. Divorces and separations are few and far in between. In fact, if there is a perceptible rise in their figures, it can be attributed to modern methods of contracting marriage by disregarding the chart and family background and banking on such trivial and worthless factors as common interests, vocational prospects and worse, assessments based on dating and frequent meetings between the two young people.

Chart 3 : Male : Born 1/2-11-1935 at 5-40 a.m. (IST) at 13N 28, 77E 23 with a-balance of 6 years, 1 month and 24 days of Venus Dasa at birth.

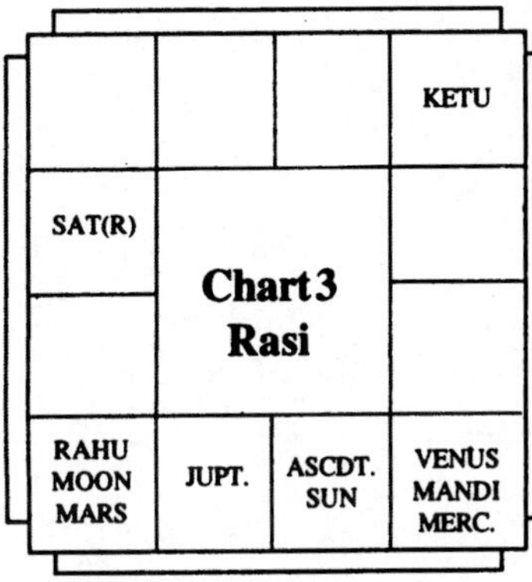

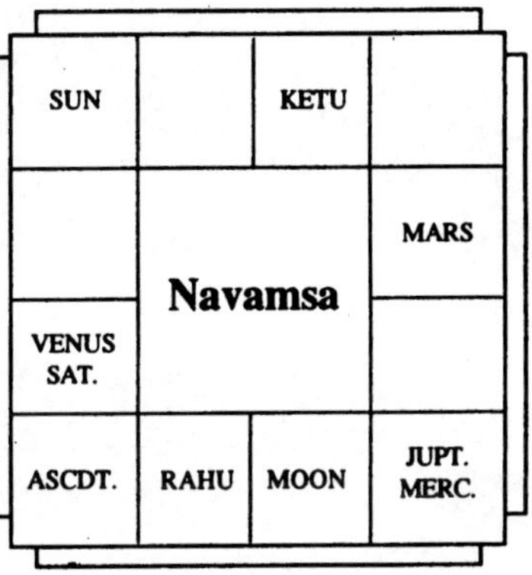

In this case (Chart 3), there is the Sun in the Lagna debilitated while the Moon is with malefics Mars and Rahu as given in combination (p). A closer look would show only malefics in Kendras and Trikonas, the Sun in the first and Saturn in the 5th. The Ascendant and 8th lord Venus is in the 12th [combination (g)]. The Moon afflicted in an Apoklima (the 3rd) and the Lagna lord in the 12th (Apoklima) with the Moon and Lagna afflicted by Rahu-Mars and the Sun respectively fulfil combination (*l*). The native consistently refused to even consider any proposals. He passed away in September 1963 after a heart attack described by the doctors as myocardial infarction. He was hale and healthy right through to the last day. ●

Chapter II

Points to Ponder

II

Matching is a long-drawn process that calls for careful scrutiny of a large number of factors. Some charts are easy to decipher ; others are knotty and tangled. As in other fields, no one should grudge a reasonable fee for the work of matching charts for marriage. Some people are aghast when a fee is quoted for the job. They complain that sometimes 10, 15 or even 150 charts have to be scrutinised before a suitable match can be found and how on earth can one afford to pay for so many cases ? This question points to the great ignorance in the minds of the public on the role of matching charts, and more importantly, of its place in the scheme of things in negotiating an alliance. **Matching, it must be emphasised in no uncertain terms, is to be reserved until all other factors of a lesser nature have been cleared.** When this is done, then the number of charts that may have to be screened dwindles to the one-digit figure and only in the rarest of rare cases does it touch two digits.

Matching is a job for the expert and an appropriate fee is only reasonable. Often, those who hesitate to pay for matching quote the ancient practice of the astrologer not charging any fee. Several classical works like **Prasna Marga, Prasna Tantra** and others start with a Sloka that calls on one to go to an astrologer laden with fruits, flowers and gold coins (fees in modern parlance) which means there is really nothing to support the argument that astrological work should be rendered free. Some people even go to the extent of saying charging fees for astrological work tends to make the predictions go awry; in other words, fees tend to affect adversely one's predictive skills. It is true that in the ancient history of our country, the concept of fees was something unknown for thousands of years, especially in the teaching, medical and astrological fields. Social conditions were such that no doctor charged a fee as it was thought his diagnostic and prognostic abilities would not function properly, if he did so much as accept a copper for his services. Likewise, it was for the teacher. Teachers took it upon themselves as a religious, spiritual and moral Dharma or duty to impart education free to the young. Not only did they charge no fees, but also took the youngsters under their wing, treating them as their own children. Sometimes, the Guru's fondness for his students even exceeded his attachment for his own sons. But no matter, how admirable such attitudes at one point of time, they cannot be emulated any more in present times. The learned — doctors, astrologers and teachers — were patronised by the kings and well-to-do who gave them vast grants of land and gifts of gold and cattle to run their institutions and their lives. This is no longer possible and unless a modest fee is charged, no professional can lead a life of independence or self-respect. The astrologer is no exception too. Grudging an astrologer his legitimate fee for the work he does speaks only of double standards. A marriage costs a fortune now-a-days with a lot of vulgar waste and extravagance thrown in. The fee charged for matching can only be described as infinitesimally minute and negligible in a marriage budget, especially, if only one ponders on and appreciates how important and invaluable, correct astrological guidance can be to the soundness and stability of the match in question.

Doctors, today, charge sums that leave many patients financially devastated. Education, even for the merit student, can cost a fortune even at school level. For others, there is also a big racket with unscrupulous pedagogues trading marks cards and degrees for brazen considerations running into lakhs of rupees. Yet, people servilely accept these trends and decline in ethical standards as a necessary part of the system and as something that cannot be questioned. No competent astrological savant can ever dream of competing with the doctor or the pedagogue in terms of the fees they charge. Nor can one dispute the superiority of the services rendered by a conscientious qualified astrologer. Of course, there may be quacks claiming to be astrologers who may fleece the gullible. They must be brought to book. Nobody disputes that. But then which discipline does not have its quota of cheats and quacks — science, medicine, law, banking, accountancy, engineering, teaching ? In every area of knowledge there are people who bring discredit to the discipline but these people are not identified with the discipline. It is only against the astrological savant, dual standards are practised and the discipline is criticised when a quack claims to be an astrologer. This is unfair to the science and matters can be set right only when astrology is introduced as a subject of serious pursuit in schools and colleges.

Often, some scientists go off at a tangent talking angrily against matching of charts saying it does not fit into the scheme of science. And if it is not science, it has to be superstition, they conclude at once. Why should it, in the first place, fit into the parameters of science ? Science is not a panacea for all the ills mankind is heir to. Science can do very little. In fact, too much of science can make one lopsided and machine-like. Just because matching cannot be explained in scientific jargon (or in terms of physics and chemistry as the rationalists would have it), one need not rush to shout from the roof-tops it is nonsense. The compositions of the great saint Thyagaraja or the benedictory words of the Paramacharya of Kanchi or the music of Mrs. Subbulakshmi have no science in them — yet they have an indescribable power over the one listening to them to bring in phenomenal changes in the heart and mind, that no doctor or scientist can either explain or bring about. Likewise, it is with matching charts. Marital tragedies and premature termination of mariages can be prevented only through astrology. No scientist or rationalist can do this kind of work.

Immature budding journalists are often known to attack matching of charts under the delusion they are omniscient. Oftentimes, newspapers carry headings such as "Match blood, not horoscopes" with stories of how an AIDS patient married and died shortly afterwards, but not before passing on the AIDS virus to his young wife. It is not clear why the unfavorable comparison to astrology is made in such newspaper stories and reports. But it is quite evident that those who write such stories do so from a point of total ignorance of the scope of matching charts and what astrology actually is. Many times, their idea of astrology is based solely on Sunday supplement forecasts which no serious student of astrology will endorse as being astrological.

In a case such as that referred to above, the horoscope could have definitely given a better picture of the whole thing. In the first place, it would have shown a serious deficiency in the longevity of the dead man and of the presence of some serious physical malady. This, in itself, would have been sufficient to have saved the young bride not only from widowhood but also from the dreaded HIV virus.

Some sections of the media and one or two members of the scientific community talk of tests carried out on couples married according to the Zodiacal signs and of couples married without reference to horoscopes facing the same levels of marital peace or unhappiness. They, therefore, conclude, horoscopic matching does not work.

There are two angles to such claims. **Firstly, no tests have ever been conducted at all as claimed by these critics. Secondly, they do not have even the faintest acquaintance with the methods of matching horoscopes as enunciated in classical works.**

The matching tests, they claim, are based on Zodiacal signs. What do these "rationalists" mean by this ? **Matching cannot be done on Zodiacal signs. This is not matching at all**. The Zodiacal signs (the Sun-signs as given in newspaper Sunday supplements) they talk about are not recognised in Jyotisha at all. No classical astrological text defines Aries as coming between April 22 and May 22 as made out by these "rationalists". Such a basis for their tests is nonsense. **How can people who are ignorant of even the basics of Jyotisha arrogate to themselves such omniscience as to talk of conducting tests in the area of matching charts ? Matching charts is the job of a highly experienced astrologer. How can those who do not even know the meaning of the Zodiacal sign or the definition of a Graha or Nakshatra claim to conduct such tests ?** It is akin to a vegetable vendor (with no academic training) questioning the Einsteinian equation $E = mc^2$. Or, it is like these "scientists" saying just because two men are of the same height, the heart of one can be transplanted to the other. Such a conclusion would be dangerous, presumptuous, foolish and arrogant and can never be acceptable to medical experts. Likewise, the claims of rationalists to be qualified to conduct tests on matching. Such claims are a sad reflection on the arrogance and foolishness of these rationalists who claim to be the repositories of "scientific temper" and "rationalism" of the land.

In fact many a time, these critics, who seem to be desperate, take recourse to crude lies. I can recall how, not once but several times, a so-called scientist-cum-science-fiction writer and also a Sunday supplement wag, neither of whom loses no opportunity to talk disparagingly of astrology, began to cook up "facts" to support their case against astrology. One of them first concocted the "proof" and the other followed suit when they began to write that a certain *Professor Bernard Silverman, psychologist at Michigan State University, got records of 2,978 married and 478 divorced couples between 1967 and 1968. He found no co-relation with astrologer's predictions. Those married under "compatible signs married and divorced just as often as those born under "incompatible" signs.* This piece of research was claimed to be based on "statistics and careful reading of birth dates in "Who's Who". Such "studies" are a mockery of the scientific temper which these rationalists profess to monopolize and show to what unethical levels they can stoop as my enquiries to locate Professor Bernard Silverman of Michigan State University ultimately proved. After reading this report, I addressed a letter dated 31-1-1995 to Prof. Bernard Silverman, Psychology Department, Michigan State University, Michigan, U.S.A. in which I wrote :

Dear Prof. Silverman,

I am interested in knowing if you have carried out any studies on astrological factors and marriages. If yes, kindly let me know if these astrological factors are based on Vedic or Hindu astrology. I would appreciate an early reply from you.

Thanking you,

Yours sincerely,
Gayatri Devi Vasudev
(Associate Editor)

The letter was posted on the same date. I was eagerly looking forward to hearing from the "Professor", but I was in for a disappointment when the letter came back to me on 25-2-1995 marked in red ink **"Not at MSU — Return to Sender".** Instead of giving up, I wrote another letter dated 18-5-1995, addressed not to the "Professor" but to the Head of the Department, Department of Psychology, Michigan State University, Michigan, U.S.A., as follows :

Dear Sir,

I would appreciate very much if you could kindly furnish the following information relating to Prof. Bernard Silverman who was said to be the Head of the Department in your University in the 1960's (?). Please clarify if he was the Head of the Psychology Department in either the late 1950's or the 1960's or at any other time. Kindly also let me know if any details of his studies (provided, he was there in the University) on astrological factors and marriages can be furnished. If he is alive and if his whereabouts are available, kindly let me have his address so that I can correspond with him direct.

Thanking you,

Yours sincerely,
Gayatri Devi Vasudev

This time happily, the letter was not returned to me by the University but elicited a reply from Professor Gordon Wood, Chairperson, Department of

Psychology, Michigan State University. His reply drove the last nail on the coffin of the concocted proof of the fiction-writer-cum-scientist. The reply is reproduced here and is dated 31-5-1995. It says :

Dear Mr. Vasudev,

I am responding to your letter of May 18th in which you ask whether Professor Bernard Silverman was ever Head of the Department of Psychology at Michigan State University.

I have never heard of Professor Bernard Silverman. He was never the Head of the Department of Psychology at Michigan State University. I was unable to find his name in the directory of the American Psychological Association. So I cannot provide you with any information about him.

Cordially,

Gordon Wood

Professor and Chairperson

Not only was there no Professor Bernard Silverman in Michigan State University but also in the whole of the United States of America. How strange !

It is pathetic an officially designated scientist of India should descend to such a level to push his prejudice against astrology. Why I cite this case is to show that nowhere has matching of charts been proved wrong, although a lot of stories are made up and floated by pseudo-rationalists to decry this traditional method of making stable and harmonious marriages. In fact, if in India, all sorts

MICHIGAN STATE UNIVERSITY

DEPARTMENT OF PSYCHOLOGY
PSYCHOLOGY RESEARCH BUILDING

EAST LANSING • MICHIGAN • [illegible]

May 31, 1995

Gayatri Devi Vasudev
Associate Editor
Raman Publications
"Sri Rajeswari", 28 Nehru Circle
Seshadripuram, Bangalore-560 020
INDIA

Dear Mr. Vasudev:

I am responding to your letter of May 18th in which you ask whether Professor Bernard Silverman was ever Head of the Department of Psychology at Michigan State University.

I have never heard of Professor Bernard Silverman. He was never the Head of the Department of Psychology at Michigan State University. I was unable to find his name in the directory of the American Psychological Association so I cannot provide you with any information about him.

Cordially,

Gordon Wood
Professor and Chairperson

of political invasions and cultural onslaughts on her have not been able to make a dent on her social fabric, the credit to a great extent, should go to the practice of horoscope matching. This method of making marital alliances has made many marriages survive all kinds of problems making the basic unit of society strong contributing thereby to the mental and moral health of generations.

Sometimes, a question is raised if matching of charts can do anything to thwart destined events and situations like unhappy marriages, divorce, separation etc. Astrology, as we understand, is only a science of tendencies and there is no such thing as absolute determinism. What matching does is to allow scope for human effort to overcome the negative indications in a chart *vis-a-vis* marital life. It is in this frame of mind that matching of charts should be done. The job of matching is not for novices for it calls for a careful assessment of several factors, not the least important being of longevity, one of the hardest nuts to crack in horoscopic delineation. The merits of horoscopic matching and its role in keeping society cohesive are now being recognised by Western societies. More and more people in the West are now veneering to matching of charts before taking their step to the altar. ●

Chapter III

Mental and Psychological Health

III

Once a chart has been cleared on the longevity count, the next step is to examine the afflictions in the chart, especially in relation to the Ascendant (showing the body) and the Moon (ruling the mind) as well as Mercury (ruling the intellect).

Afflictions to the Moon and Mercury, if strong, result in severe psychological complexes that could affect normal life.

Heavy afflictions to the Moon have a two-fold significance.

Depending upon the rest of the chart, the afflictions to the Moon can adversely affect longevity. If this does not happen, then the native becomes a case for a psychologist. Such natives may display normal social behaviour ; but deep underneath, they are cauldrons of serious emotional disturbances and psychological complexes. Such natives can make life miserable for those they marry. Depending upon the intensity or nature of affliction, they can either be schizophrenic, paranoid, neurotic or even homicidal. If the affliction is from Saturn, such natives suffer from excessive melancholy or depression and living with them can impair severely the peace of the family. They suffer from a persecution complex and believe they are martyrs in life and that everyone should be beholden to them; otherwise, they go haywire.

Afflictions centering on the Moon from Mars make for violent moods, behaviour and action. They are very harsh in speech and can lash with their tongues with such ferocity, their victims may soon end up as mental wrecks.

If the Moon is afflicted by Rahu, then one suffers from dangerous levels of suspicion and homicidal tendencies.

If the Moon is with Ketu, the native suffers from an intense inferiority complex, clams up and withdraws into a shell. The escape route that appeals to such natives is self-destruction or suicide. Otherwise, there may be a great longing for spiritual life.

If the Moon is afflicted by two or more of these malefics — Saturn, Mars, afflicted Mercury, Rahu, Sun or Ketu — then, whatever the other merits of the chart, one is safe by staying away from such individuals.

In all these cases of affliction to the Moon, the aspect or association of Jupiter, Venus or the sign-dispositer tends to tone down the affliction considerably, when the chart can be considered if other factors are favorable.

When a Moon - Mercury combination occurs, involving the watery signs, especially Pisces or Scorpio where Mercury and the Moon are respectively in debility, we have demonic natures cloaked in an apparently attractive exterior. Such natives can harbour horrendous levels of avarice, hate, jealousy and other morbid emotions that can lead to ruin, death and depravity.

A simple looking woman who could easily pass off for a quiet, docile but friendly type, the native of

Chart 4 possessed an insatiable lust for money. This woman was convicted for several murders and sentenced to death.

She married after high school and had 3 children.

Chart 4 : Born 4-4-1943 at 19h. 10m. (ZST) at 34 N 18, 99 W 44 with a balance of 7 years, 8 months and 17 days of Mercury Dasa.

SUN 22-44 MOON 23-57 MERC. 23-26	VENUS 25-26	SAT. 16-52	JUPT. 24-23
KETU 0-55	**Chart 4 Rasi**		
MARS 29-00			RAHU 0-55
			LAGNA 12-46

	ASCDT. RAHU	JUPT.	SAT.
MOON MERC.	**Navamsa**		
SUN			
	VENUS	KETU	MARS

The husband died on 15-5-1971, when she collected a huge sum on insurance. Thereafter, she collected fire insurance money on 2 houses that got burnt.

In January 1978, she moved in with a new boy-friend. In May 1980, a son died in a drowning accident. In June 1980, another son survived lead and arsenic poisoning when the whole truth came tumbling out. All the accidents and deaths were engineered by the woman with an eye on the insurance money.

Virgo rising is aspected by the Lagna lord Mercury, the Sun and the Moon. Mercury is in very close conjunction with the Sun and the Moon. The Moon is New. This combination involving the Lagna lord made her a heartless killer who meticulously planned each killing to look like an accident.

One of the best things to have in a chart for a marital alliance is a Moon, free of associations. Such individuals carry the traits of the sign occupied by the Moon. These traits may be good or bad, but their intensity is in control and can be easily diffused. For example,

(a) The Moon in Aries can make one assertive and impulsive but also frank.

(b) The Moon in Taurus gives a stable mind but a streak of obstinacy cannot be ruled out.

(c) The Moon in Gemini gives duplicity but within safe levels. It also gives an intellectual leaning.

(d) The Moon in Cancer makes one emotional and utterly concerned with the needs of those around them.

(e) The Moon in Leo shows up as a somewhat egoistic nature but gives a positive and sunny disposition.

(f) The Moon in Virgo gives practicality and an eye for detail but it can make one extremely sensitive.

(g) The Moon in Libra gives a vascillating mind that can have difficulty in making decisions and fickleness but can make one affectionate also.

(h) The Moon in Scorpio gives a capacity for loving others and deep loyalties but a touchy nature.

(i) The Moon in Sagittarius is a blessing. Broad-mindedness and respect for the feelings of others characterise the native.

(j) The Moon in Capricorn gives a friendly nature and an ability to do anything well to the minutest detail. But there is also an obsession for perfection.

(k) The Moon in Aquarius gives a reserved, serious nature. Though not friendly, they are humane.

(l) The Moon in Pisces gives a large heart and a loving nature but marked by changeability.

All these traits are in themselves desirable in life. Depending upon the association of the Moon with benefics or malefics, the positive traits may get enhanced or the negative ones may get aggravated.

The Moon with Venus gives a friendly nature, whatever the sign occupied by the Moon. The natives are amicable, fond of beauty or aesthetics and have an ability to share happiness. They are optimistic.

Jupiter with the Moon is also always welcome and gives a great magnanimity of mind and heart that can easily forgive. Irrespective of the sign, these streaks flavor the native's mental disposition. Depending upon the nature of the signs and the house occupied by the Moon, the expression of these characteristics may vary.

The Moon in the 6th (house of sickness), 8th (house of sins) or the 12th (the house of loss or weakness) tends to get weakened and can create a mindset that is not healthy in attitude. However, the Moon even if in these houses, but aspected by benefics or endowed with digital strength overcomes the deficiency he would otherwise suffer from.

The following combinations point to deficiencies in mental health and depending upon the strength of the rest of the horoscope, can either get diffused or get sufficiently aggravated to varying degrees and manifest in the form of abnormal behaviour and moods :

(1) Jupiter in the Ascendant and Mars in the 7th.

An Aries native with Jupiter in the 1st and Mars in the 7th was capable of extreme cruelty and terrorised all the members of the household.

(2) Saturn in the Ascendant while Mars is in the 6th, 8th or 12th from Saturn.

(3) Saturn in Lagna, the Sun in the 12th, the Moon or Mars in a trine.

(4) The 3rd lord eclipsed (in conjunction with Rahu or Ketu) or in depression or in the 6th house aspected by a malefic — madness caused through poison.

For example, for Aries Lagna, if Mercury is with Rahu or in Pisces or in Virgo and is at the same time aspected by Saturn, it causes a predisposition to mental and psychological abnormalities.

(5) The waning Moon and Saturn in the 12th.

Such a combination produces psychopathic behaviour when one becomes capable of glib social behaviour while at the same time one can be subject to moods of great hate, violence and self-pity leading to severe aberrational behaviour.

(6) If Saturn and the 2nd lord conjoin malefics :

a. Saturn and the 2nd lord with the Sun,
b. Saturn and the 2nd lord with Mars,
c. Saturn and the 2nd lord with Rahu and
d. Saturn and the 2nd lord with afflicted Mercury.

(7) The Moon and Saturn aspected by Mercury who should be in the Ascendant.

(8) If the Moon be eclipsed and posited in Lagna and malefics occupy the trines, the native becomes demonic — malevolent, wicked, diabolical.

(9) If a malefic be in the 4th and the 4th lord be

associated with another malefic, an hostile mind and wickedness would result.

(10) Saturn in the Ascendant and Mars in the 5th, 7th or the 9th.

(11) The Moon and Mercury combust in the Ascendant.

(12) Weak Moon associated with a malefic in the Ascendant, the 5th, 8th or 9th houses.

(13) Mandi in the 7th conjunct a malefic.

(14) Afflicted Mercury in the 3rd, 6th, 8th or 12th.

These combinations, if present in a chart, are to be carefully analysed. Exonerating factors such as a strong Ascendant, the Moon or Mercury or the influence of natural benefics must be identified carefully. If such factors are present and the Dasas are also favorable, then the afflictions may be deemed to be ineffectual. However, if no redeeming factors are present, charts with such combinations must be put aside as being unsafe for peace in marriage as well as for containing explosive material at the mental and psychological levels.

Chart 5, of a man accused and arrested for the violent murder of his wife, makes an interesting example in this context.

The Ascendant is Gemini whose ruler Mercury is in the 4th in his sign of exaltation with the Sun.

The Ascendant is occupied by the Moon and Rahu. Both the Ascendant and the Moon are in Aridra ruled by Rahu. Saturn, a powerful malefic, is retrograde in the 9th, a trine. Combination (8) is present in part.

Both the Ascendant and the Moon are afflicted by

the Nodal axis. The afflicted Moon in the Ascendant and Mercury are in Kendras. The Moon has no favorable aspects. Mercury is, somewhat, helped by

Chart 5 : Born 28-9-1964 at 23h. at 13 N 49, 76 E 32 with a balance of 6 years, 8 months and 22 days of Rahu Dasa at birth.

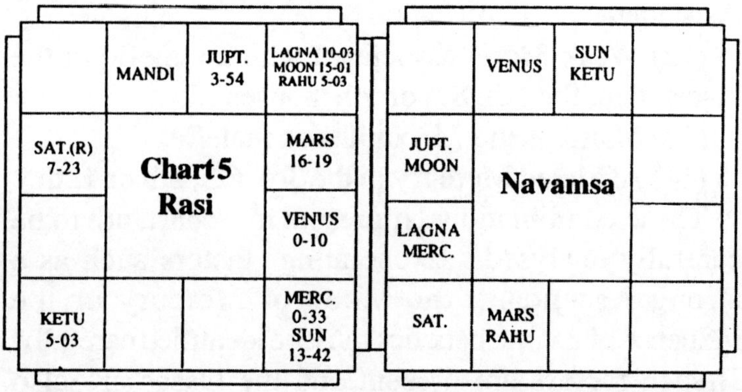

Jupiter's aspect. But as both the Ascendant and the Moon are heavily afflicted,one should be wary of such a chart rejecting it even before taking up the matching proper. Events after the marriage in the case of Chart 5 justify the astrological factors of aberrational mental behaviour and health. ●

Chapter IV

More than One Marriage

IV

After one is through with an examination of longevity and sound mental health, the next step is to look for factors that show more than one marriage. Where a combination for such an event is present, it implies the chances of the marriage surviving are feeble and therefore, matching tests must be carried out with great care and thoroughness. It may not be only a second marriage that is indicated, it could also indicate extra-marital flings and liaisons (subject to other planetary features) which could therefore, disqualify the chart in the first place. Where marriage is deemed a sacrament as in our country, the boy and girl, both pure in body and mind, are brought together to live a life of peace, purity and Dharma. And, therefore, combinations that can hurt marriage must be carefully identified. Yogas for more than one marriage are to be carefully looked into before disqualifying the chart. But it is important to remember that the *more than one marriage result* can apply to either the native or the spouse (and not necessarily to the native alone) and this can be deciphered only after assessing the chart from different angles.

The following combinations, unless modified by other factors, show more than one marriage :

(1) When the 7th lord is combust (by his proximity to the Sun), debilitated (without cancellation) or very weak in an inimical sign.

(2) The 7th lord afflicted by malefics in a malefic sign or debilitated and if Mercury or Saturn be in the 7th.

(3) If Mars, Venus and Saturn occupy the 7th and the Lagna lord be in the 8th.

(4) If Venus occupies a common sign and the ruler of this sign occupies his exaltation sign and the 7th lord is weak.

(5) If the Lagna lord and the 7th lord as well as Karaka Venus occupy dual signs.

These combinations apply equally well to both male and female charts and show more than one marriage in the absence of exonerating factors.

In Chart 6, the Ascendant is Aries. The 7th lord Venus is in the 6th in a common sign with the aspect of 11th lord Saturn and Lagna lord Mars. While the aspect of Mars being that of the Lagna lord cannot be faulted, the aspect of malefic Saturn on the Kalatrakaraka Venus (in this case, the 7th lord as well) in a dual sign must be viewed with some reservation. More than one marriage being indicated, the chart does not pass the test of matching.

Chart 6: Female : Born 21-8-1930 at 9-22 p.m. at 3 W O, 51 N 3 with a balance of 17 years, 6 months and 27 days of Saturn Dasa.

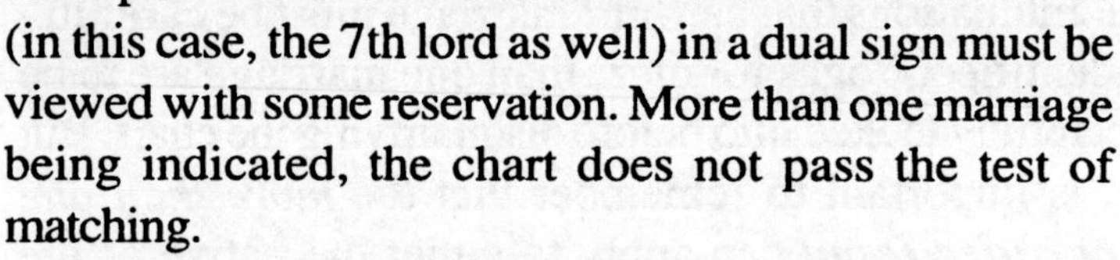

After being married for 10 years with 2 children, the couple separated in 1976 with the divorce coming in 1978.

A more-than-one marriage combination in a chart can indicate that the first marriage may not last for one reason or the other. It need not necessarily imply profligacy or extra-marital associations. However, in cases of those who have lost their spouses to death or due to divorce and are seeking a second marriage, the chart has to be reviewed from this angle also and then approved.

(6) If the 8th lord be in the 1st or the 7th.

The native of Chart 7 married in October 1979. His wife delivered a baby boy by caesarean section on 9-9-1991 and expired on 15-10-1991. The native then married a widow on 25-4-1993.

Chart 7: Born 7-3-1953 at 7-15 p.m. at 31 N 30, 75 E 40 with a balance of 8 years, 7 months and 22 days of Saturn Dasa at birth.

MARS MERC.	VENUS JUPT.		
SUN	**Chart 7 Rasi**		RAHU
KETU			
	MOON	SAT.(R)	ASCDT.

MARS		VENUS SUN	KETU
ASCDT.	**Navamsa**		
RAHU	SAT. JUPT.	MOON MERC.	

This chart has the Lagna lord in the 7th in a common sign joined by malefic Mars. Mars as 8th lord in the 7th can show more than one marriage. The 7th lord Jupiter in the 8th is also not favorable for the first marriage and its durability.

(7) If the Lagna lord be in the 6th.

(8) If the 2nd lord be in the 6th and if a malefic occupies the 7th.

(9) If the 7th lord along with a benefic occupies an inimical sign or his sign of debilitation and the 7th house is occupied by a malefic.

(10) If the significator of spouse, namely, Venus be with a malefic or occupy a sign of depression or inimical sign or eclipsed Navamsa.

(11) If 3 or more malefics occupy the 7th house.

(12) If 3 or more malefics are in the 2nd house and are not aspected by the 2nd lord.

(13) Three or more malefics in the 7th if not aspected by the 7th lord.

(14) If malefics occupy the 1st, the 2nd and the 7th houses and the 7th lord is in the 1st in his debility, inimical sign or eclipsed.

(15) If the Lagna is occupied by an exalted planet or the lord of the Lagna is himself exalted.

(16) If the Moon and Venus are strong and in conjunction.

(17) If the 1st, 2nd and 6th lords be conjoined with malefics and occupy the 7th.

(18) If the 7th lord Saturn be joined by a malefic.

(19) If a powerful Moon occupy the 3rd house from the 7th lord.

(20) If the 2nd and 12th lords be in the 3rd and be aspected by the 9th lord or Jupiter.

(21) If the 7th lord is strong in a quadrant or trine and in a benefic Varga aspected by the 10th lord.

(22) If the 7th and 11th lords be in conjunction or in mutual aspect.

(23) If the ruler of the Navamsa occupied by the 7th lord be joined by a benefic and is in Parvata or higher Vargas and otherwise strong.

(24) If the 7th lord be weak and the 7th house be aspected by or conjoined with a malefic.

Chart 8: Born 23-8-1952 at 9-14 p.m. at 12N18, 76E39 with a balance of 8 years, 7 months and 28 days of Moon Dasa at birth.

ASCDT.	JUPT.		
	Chart 8		MERC.
RAHU			SUN
	MARS		MOON SAT.

KETU	MOON		SUN
ASCDT.	**Navamsa**		SAT.
MERC.			MARS
JUPT.	VENUS		RAHU

In Chart 8, the 7th and 5th lords Mercury and the Moon respectively, have exchanged signs. The 7th house is a common sign with the Moon in it joined by malefic Saturn. Additionally, Saturn here is the 11th lord too. The native married in March 1990. In 1995, the husband started an affair with a girl he met at the place of his work. In January 1998, he moved into a new house with this girl and they even had a child. Combination 24 applies to Chart 8 but unfortunately, in a different way. In this case, the spouse proved unfaithful and had another wife (?) even while his marriage with the native continued. The point in such cases is not who gets into an extra-marital affair or relationship, but how the affliction can damage marital fidelity and peace. Therefore, when such a case as Chart 8 is brought up for comparison, it would be better to avoid it than get caught in unhappy marital complications.

A predominance of common signs with the Ascendant, the Moon, the Ascendant lord, the 7th lord and Venus occupying them is a clear indication of marital life going awry due to a break up of the relationship. It may be due to the native or the spouse and this depends upon the rest of the chart. The break up may result from a third party trespassing into the marriage, but not necessarily for this reason always. The marriage may not necessarily end in divorce, but for all practical reasons, it may prove totally disillusioning. In Chart 8, the spouse has not divorced the native who continues to live with her in-laws who are sympathetic to her plight, but helpless. The spouse spends all his time and money on the other woman and rarely visits his wife.

Such combinations are a primary indication of the marriage being destroyed. In certain cases, this may follow from the native's own death where the chart may not show good longevity. In a case, with Virgo rising and the Moon (11th lord) in the 7th in Pisces, the Kendras were all afflicted by malefics. The native, with a loving wife and two kids, suddenly succumbed to a massive heart attack when just 42 years old. His marriage ended with his early death; so did the marriage of his wife opening up the possibility of a second marriage for her. This defect was not identified in the husband's chart before marriage leading to premature termination of the match due to death.

(25) If the 2nd lord be weak and the 2nd house is occupied or aspected by a malefic, the native will have another wife while the first is living.

(26) If the lords of the 1st and the 7th houses be in debility, inimical or eclipsed Navamsa, the native will have another wife while the first is living.

(27) If malefics occupy the 7th and 8th houses and Mars be in the 12th house, the native will have another wife while the first is living.

All these combinations have to be carefully assessed before concluding that the chart has more than one marriage. Where such a combination is present and there is a favorable aspect of Jupiter, the Lagna lord or the sign-dispositer, then in such a case the combination may get checked and disallow more than one spouse. These combinations, although according to classical works are said to denote more than one wife, can also be extended to imply more than one husband in female charts. These combinations can cover cases of extra-marital relationships which may not necessarily fit into the definition of a second wife or husband. **However, one must note, such combinations need not necessarily show more than one spouse.** They can imply the marriage, the first one — which is usually the only one in most parts of India — may face danger of breaking up due to death or divorce of spouse. Such combinations should be assessed against the background of the entire chart and no single isolated combination should be taken as conclusive.

Certain other combinations show loyal and faithful spouses and if present in one chart can counter-balance the indication for more than one association in the other chart. For example, if the Moon and Jupiter occupy the 7th sign from the Karakamsa in Navamsa, then it shows a loyal, devoted spouse. The Karakamsa is the sign occupied by the Atmakaraka in Navamsa.

If the 7th lord be in the 4th or the 10th house, then the spouse will be devoted to the native.

If the 7th lord or the Karaka Venus be conjoined with or aspected by a benefic or be placed between benefics, the spouse will be good and faithful.

If Jupiter occupy the 7th house, then also it gives a good spouse.

If the 7th lord or the 7th house be conjoined with or aspected by Jupiter and is also strong, it gives a good partner.

If the Sun is the 7th lord and is aspected by a benefic, the native's spouse will be devoted to the native.

If Venus as 7th lord be aspected by a benefic, it shows a devoted spouse.

If the 7th lord be in a Kendra in a benefic Navamsa conjoined with or aspected by a benefic, a loyal partner is shown.

If the 7th house is aspected by Jupiter, then also it shows a devoted spouse.

In a general sense, the 7th house either from the Lagna or the Moon conjoined with or aspected

by a benefic or the lord of that sign gives marital peace, fidelity and stability. In other words, it can stave off the situation of breaking up a marriage. ●

Chapter V

Dosha Samya
or
Balancing of Malefic Content

V

Once the mental and psychological health of a native is confirmed as normal against the background of longevity and dual marriage ruled out, we then move on to an assessment of the Bhavas related to personal happiness. These Bhavas are the 2nd (Kutumbastana), the 4th (Sukastana), the 7th (Kalatrastana), the 8th (Mangalyastana) and the 12th (Sayanasukastana). No chart can be totally devoid of afflictions. Every chart has a certain quanta of Doshas. But it cannot be discarded on this count.

The Ascendant afflicted by malefics in certain respects also points to a life of great suffering and therefore, indirectly has a bearing on the quality or quantum of marital life.

A careful examination of the Dosha content of each chart is to be made and if a similar quantum of Dosha is found in the other, then the two can be paired with impunity. There are certain Doshas that are more potent than others. These have to be paired with like Doshas if they should be diffused and rendered ineffective.

Mars is a planet of aggression, violence and ill-will. Therefore, his occupation of the Bhavas listed above breeds these evils in the relevant sectors of life causing great anguish and suffering to one. One may, therefore, be deprived of marital harmony due to the cruelty of the spouse or in-laws or because of hostility in the marital environment.

Saturn is the chronic trouble-maker and stands for all that is associated with drudgery, long-drawn illness, manipulatory tactics, indifference or aversion. So, when Saturn occupies the Ascendant, the 2nd, the 4th, the 7th, the 8th or the 12th, he brings these factors into play in the personal life of an individual marring conjugal felicity.

The Sun rules the ego and his presence in houses related to marital life leads to ego conflicts, extremely high-handed and arrogant behaviour patterns and issues of prestige and social standing as well as a degree of cruelty (the Sun being a Kruri or cruel planet) surfacing as a blot on marital peace.

Rahu and Ketu stand for explosiveness and clamming respectively and, in relevant houses, can lead to explosive situations revolving around infidelity, sodomy, perversions, impotency, frigidity, bickerings and domination from destructive elements in the family with the sum result marital life gets blighted.

These results are not absolute but factors indicating them must never be overlooked in finalising a marital alliance. They must be identified carefully and then made ineffective by similar factors in the other chart.

Of all the Doshas, coming under this head, the more dangerous are those caused by Mars or Rahu in the 7th or the 8th. Rahu in the 4th is also to be handled cautiously.

Mars in the 2nd, 4th or 12th is relatively less malevolent, so also Rahu in the 2nd and 12th.

Mars and Saturn in the 1st house can be disastrous depending upon the Lagna and the Chandra Lagna involved.

If the Lagna is Aries, Cancer, Leo, Virgo, Scorpio, Sagittarius or Pisces, Saturn in the Lagna, unless qualified by other factors, can give a life of trial and tribulation and especially, if the 7th house factors are weak, loss of spouse. Even here, Saturn in Aries, Cancer and Pisces seems to be more damaging than in Leo, Virgo, Scorpio and Sagittarius.

Mars in the 1st, on the other hand, becomes highly inimical for marital happiness if in Taurus, Gemini or Virgo or Scorpio. As always, benefic influences tone down the maleficence that goes with Mars in these signs as Ascendants.

The following pairs of charts are a good illustration of the bad matching of charts.

The girl (Chart 9) got married on 15-5-1993 and within 3 months, the marriage broke up. All efforts at reconciliation failed and the couple separated.

Chart 9 has the following afflictions :

(1) Mars (R) in the 8th from Lagna;

Chart 9 : Female: Born 28-9-1973 at 5-10 a.m. at 16 N 13, 81 E 12.

	MARS (R)		SAT. KETU
	Chart 9 **Rasi** **Female** **AWW-03-'97**		
JUPT.(R)			
RAHU		MERC. VENUS	ASCDT. SUN MOON

	SUN JUPT.	VENUS	RAHU
	Navamsa		
ASCDT. SAT.			MARS
KETU		MERC.	MOON

Chart 10 : Male: Born 18-03-1972 at 9-04 a.m. at 16 N 59, 82 E 20.

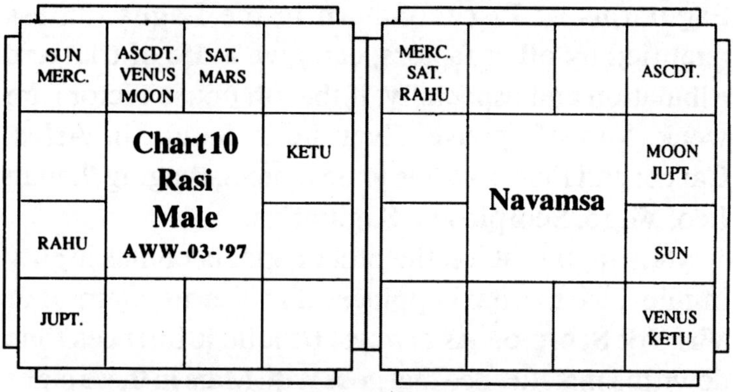

(2) Rahu in the 4th from Lagna;
(3) Mars (R) in the 8th from the Moon;
(4) Rahu in the 4th from the Moon;
(5) Mars (R) in the 7th from Venus; and
(6) The Sun in the 12th from Venus.

What are the factors that cause Dosha in the boy's case (Chart 10) ? They are :

(1) Mars in the 2nd from Lagna;
(2) Saturn in the 2nd from Lagna;
(3) Saturn in the 2nd from Venus;
(4) Mars in the 2nd from Venus;
(5) Mars in the 2nd from the Moon; and
(6) Saturn in the 2nd from the Moon.

The afflictions in the girl's chart centering on the 4th, 7th and 8th houses are far more weighty than those in the boy's chart which are all cluttered around the 2nd house. No wonder, the marriage did not work.

Therefore, where a chart has Dosha due to Mars in the 7th or 8th from either Lagna, the Moon or

Venus, it would be better to look for a similar placement of Mars in the other chart. For a girl with Mars in the 8th, it is better the boy too has Mars in the 8th. But if the girl has Mars in the 7th, Mars in the 7th or 8th for the boy would be quite okay.

Chart 11: Female: Born 05-11-1959 at 6-35 a.m.

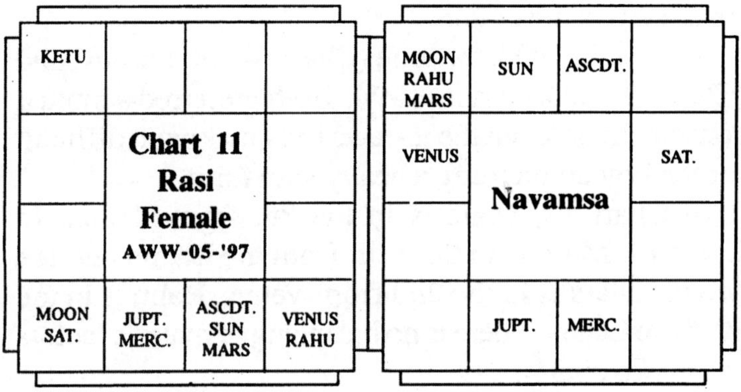

Chart 12: Male: Born 05-11-1950 at 9-30 a.m.

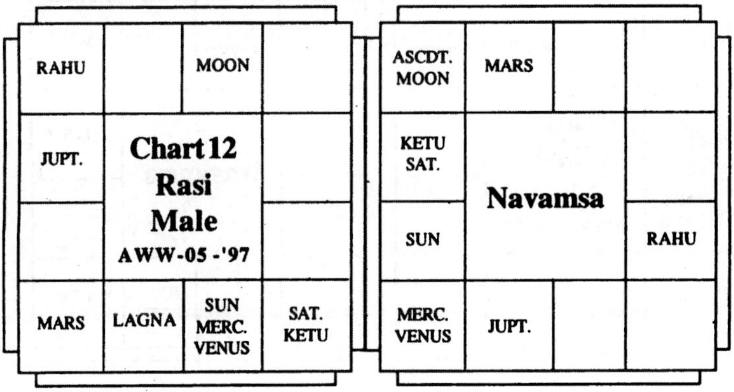

Mars in the 2nd, 4th or 12th from the Lagna, the Moon or Venus in one chart cannot really keep the Dosha caused by Mars in the 7th or 8th from Lagna, the Moon or Venus in the other chart at bay.

The boy (Chart 12) has Mars in the 8th from the Moon.

In the girl's (Chart 11), Mars and the Sun in the 2nd from Venus are no match for the boy's Dosha. Marriage for the girl is miserable.

Married in 1994, the wife (Chart 14) left the husband (Chart 13) in December 1994. Both preferred a mutual consent divorce but the in-laws tried making it difficult for the boy demanding a heavy sum for it.

In Chart 13, Mars is in the 8th from Lagna. In Chart 14, Mars is in the 12th from the Lagna and the Moon. Mars is in the 2nd from Venus, Rahu is in the 8th from Lagna. There is no balancing of malefic factors in the two charts.

Chart 13: Male: Born 31-12-1965 at 18h.16m. IST at 30 N 6, 78 E 10.

MOON		RAHU	ASCDT. JUPT.(R)
SAT.	**Chart 13 Rasi Male** AWW-10-'97		
MARS VENUS			
SUN	MERC. KETU		

MERC.	SAT. RAHU	MARS	ASCDT.
	Navamsa		VENUS
MOON			
		JUPT. KETU	SUN

A good example of absence of Dosha Samya or balancing of malefic content in the two charts is of a

Chart 14: Female: Born 23-03-1972 at 12-54 p.m. at 30 N 19, 78 E 03.

SUN MERC.(R)	VENUS	MARS SAT.	ASCDT. MOON
	Chart 14 Rasi Female		KETU
RAHU			
JUPT			

SAT.	RAHU	MOON	ASCDT.
MARS MERC.	Navamsa		
			JUPT.
	VENUS	SUN KETU	

young girl (Chart 15) married to a boy (Chart 16) overseas, both hailing from respectable families with affluent backgrounds. The girl got married and went abroad to join her husband. Once there, she underwent continuing mental torture from him. She even had to

Chart 15: Female: Born 15-07-1969 at 00-30 a.m. (IST) at 13 N, 77 E 35.

RAHU	ASCDT. SAT.	VENUS	MERC.
	Chart 15 Rasi Female		SUN MOON
	MARS		JUPT. KETU

JUPT.	MERC.	VENUS	ASCDT.
	Navamsa		SUN MOON RAHU
KETU			SAT.
		MARS	

flee to a family friend's house when she could no longer take it. From there, she came back home to India to her parents and filed for divorce on grounds of mental cruelty. The divorce was granted.

Afflictions are to be identified by malefics Sun, Mars, Saturn, Rahu or Ketu occupying the 2nd (*Kutumba* or family), the 4th (Suka or domestic environment), the 7th (*Kalatra* or spouse), the 8th (*Mạngalya* or the marital bond) and the 12th house (*Sayanasuka* or conjugal life).

There is Mars in the 8th from the Ascendant and in the 7th from the Kalatrakaraka or natural significator of spouse, Venus. The Sun occupies the 4th from the Lagna. These are the main drawbacks of Chart 15. Additionally, debilitated Saturn is in the Ascendant which, in itself, only aggravates the already existing Dosha caused by Mars and the Sun. Rahu is in the 12th from the Ascendant.

Mars occupies the 6th from the Ascendant, the 10th from the Moon and the 1st from Venus in Chart 16. In any case, he does not afflict the 2nd, 4th, 7th, 8th or

Chart 16: Male : Born 15-11-1965 at 11-15 a.m. at 13 N, 77 E 35.

MOON		RAHU	JUPT.(R)
SAT.(R)	Chart 16 Rasi		ASCDT.
MARS VENUS	MERC. KETU	SUN	

SAT.	SUN MARS	RAHU	VENUS
	Navamsa		
JUPT.	KETU	MERC.	MOON ASCDT.

the 12th from either the Ascendant, the Moon or Venus.

The Sun is in the 4th from the Ascendant in debility which is an affliction. Saturn is in the 8th from the Ascendant and in the 12th from the Moon. But the more potent affliction from Mars does not touch any of the relevant houses either from the Ascendant or the Moon or Venus. Ketu occupies the 12th from Venus.

Therefore, the balancing in malefic content between the two charts or Dosha Samya is lacking. Although Saturn in the husband's chart is in the 8th from the Ascendant, it is not sufficient to balance the strong affliction generated by Mars in the 8th from the Ascendant and the 7th from Venus in the girl's chart. Therefore, the difficulties in the marriage reached a stage of no-repair until divorce was seen as the only way out.

Where the Doshas or afflictions centering round the 2nd, 4th, 7th, 8th and 12th are quite strong and no balancing of these afflictions is made while matching, then the Doshas can take the shape of much suffering, dowry deaths, emotional alienation and physical separation or betrayal or even premature loss of spouse due to death or divorce. ●

Chapter VI

Kuta Agreement

Kuta agreement is based on the Nakshatra occupied by the Moon in the two charts. The Moon is described as Manahkaraka and naturally this test looks at the mental compatibility of the two people. But it does not stop here. There are various levels of relating between the husband and wife apart from the mental. The Kuta tests take a deeper look at the compatibility between the two —psychological, spiritual, physical, sub-conscious and sometimes, it would seem they take into cognizance compatibility at the level of blood also. Although modern medicine has evolved its own categories of blood groups and their matching, astrology also seems to take this into account at an even more subtle or refined level. For example, in many cases where the Nadi factor has not been properly matched, the marriage has experienced still-births, miscarriages as well as abortions and birth of blue-babies. This would imply the Nadi factor takes cognizance of the physical matching or genetic compatibility between the couple at a level deeper than the modern concept of blood groups.

This test of Kuta agreement takes into account 10 factors : (1) Dina, (2) Gana, (3) Mahendra, (4) Stree Deergha, (5) Yoni, (6) Rasi, (7) Rasyadhipati, (8) Vashya, (9) Rajju and (10) Vedha.

According to certain other works there are 8 factors :

(1) Varna, (2) Vashya, (3) Tara, (4) Yoni, (5) Grahamaitra, (6) Gana, (7) Bhakoota or Rasi Kuta and (8) Nadi.

Each of these factors is given 1 point more than the previous one. Varna gets **1** point, Vashya is **2**, Tara is **3**, Yoni is **4**, Grahamaitra is **5**, Gana is **6**, Bhakoota or Rasi Kuta is **7** and Nadi is **8**, totalling up to 36 points.

Rajju has not been assigned any specific value but if we go by the rule of assigning 1 point extra for each succeeding factor, Rajju should get 9 points and the total would work out to 45 points. However, since there is no mention of assigning numerical value to Rajju, we will leave it at that. However, Rajju being important, it would help the match if Rajju Kuta too is present.

If the total of the Kutas works out to 18 or more, it is said to pass the Kuta test. The greater the score, the better the compatibility.

Varna

The 12 Rasis are classed under the 4 Varnas or castes as follows :

Pisces, Scorpio and Cancer —Brahmin
Aries, Leo and Sagittarius — Kshatriya
Taurus, Virgo and Capricorn —Vaisya
Gemini, Aquarius and Libra —Sudra

A girl belonging to a higher Varna than that of the boy is not approved. Both belonging to the same Varna or the girl belonging to one lower than that of the boy is approved.

But the deficiency in the absence of Varna is made up if the ruler of the sign occupied by the Moon of the girl belongs to a Varna lower than that of the ruler of the sign occupied by the boy's Moon.

The Varnas of the planets are as follows:

Sun	—	Kshatriya
Moon	—	Vaisya
Mars	—	Kshatriya
Mercury	—	Sudra
Jupiter	—	Brahmin
Venus	—	Brahmin
Saturn	—	Sudra

For example, the Varna factor fails if the boy belongs to Aries and the girl to Scorpio as the girl would be of a higher Varna than the boy. But on checking the rulers of these two signs, we find, it is Mars for both bringing both under Kshatriya which is allowed.

The score for Varna is **1** point.

Vashya

This factor shows the mutual attraction between the two. The Janma Rasis (Moon-sign) of the groom and the girl belonging to the same group as shown here ensure harmony.

Leo and Scorpio	— Aries
Cancer and Libra	— Taurus
Virgo	— Gemini
Scorpio and Sagittarius	— Cancer
Libra	— Leo
Gemini and Pisces	— Virgo
Capricorn	— Libra
Virgo and Cancer	— Scorpio
Pisces	— Sagittarius
Aquarius and Aries	— Capricorn
Aries	— Aquarius
Capricorn	— Pisces.

Example : If the boy's Janma Rasi is Leo and the girl's Taurus, there is no Vashya Kuta. The score is **0** points.

Example : If the boy's Janma Rasi is Leo and the girl's is Aries, then Vashya Kuta may be said to be present. The score is **2** points.

If both boy and girl belong to the same sign, Vashya Kuta does not obtain:

Example : Boy — Scorpio Girl — Scorpio

Vashya is lacking.

Dina (Tara)

Count the Nakshatras from that of the bride to that of the groom and divide it by **9**. If the remainder is 2, 4, 6, 8, or 0 then it is good.

Example : If the boy's Nakshatra is Anuradha and the girl's is Rohini, counting from the girl's to the boy's, we get 14:

$$\frac{14}{9} = 1 \textit{ (Quotient)} + 5 \textit{ (Remainder)}$$

Since the remainder is 5, it is not good.

The score for Dina is **0**.

Example : If the boy's Nakshatra is Jyeshta and the girl's is Pubba — counting from the girl's constellation Poorvaphalguni to that of the boy, Jyeshta, we get 8. Since this figure is less than 9, it is to be taken as it is. Therefore, Dina Kuta is present and the score is **3** points.

Yoni Kuta

This factor takes into account the physical appetite of each Nakshatra and classifies all the 27 Nakshatras into Yonis belonging to different animals as follows :

Male	Female	Nature of Yoni
Aswini	Satabhisha	horse
Bharani	Revati	elephant
Pushya	Krittika	sheep
Rohini	Mrigasira	snake
Aslesha	Punarvasu	cat
Makha	Purvaphalguni	rat
Uttaraphalguni	Uttarabhadra	cow
Swati	Hasta	buffalo
Visakha	Chitta	tiger
Jyeshta	Anuradha	deer
Moola	Aridra	dog
Purvashada	Sravana	monkey
Purvabhadrapada	Dhanishta	lion
Uttarashada		mongoose

Nakshatras belonging to the same group are desirable. Nakshatras belonging to different groups but not ruled by animals hostile to each other are passable, while Nakshatras belonging to hostile groups are to be avoided.

Rohini and Mrigasira both belong to the *snake* group and are desirable. But Rohini and Makha belonging respectively to the *snake* and *rat* come under hostile categories and are not good. Rohini and Jyeshta belong respectively to the *snake* and *deer* categories and are passable as a pair.

The score allotted to Yoni is **4**. If the Yonis belong

to the passable category, the score is between **2** and **3**, depending upon the specific Yonis involved. If the pair belong to hostile categories, the score is **0**.

Grahamaitra

The Janma Rasi (Moon-sign) is ruled by a planet. If there is friendship (Naisargika or permanent) between the rulers of the Janma Rasis of the boy and the girl, harmony is said to prevail.

If the boy's Rasi is Taurus and that of the girl is Aquarius, then Grahamaitra is said to obtain as the rulers of these signs, Venus and Saturn respectively, are friends.

The score allotted is **5**.

If one planet is friendly and the other, neutral, then it is **4** points.

If both are neutrals, it is **3.**

If one is a friend and the other, an enemy, it is **2**.

If one is a neutral and the other, an enemy, or both are inimical, **0.**

Example : If the boy's Rasi is Aries and the girl's is Cancer, the Rasi lord of the boy Mars is *neutral* to the girl's Moon-sign lord Moon. But the girl's Moon-sign lord Moon is *friendly* to Mars, the boy's Moon-sign lord. The score would be **4** points.

Example : If the boy's Rasi is Virgo and the girl's is Sagittarius, the girl's Moon-sign lord Jupiter is *neutral* to Mercury, the boy's Moon-sign lord. On the other hand, Mercury (the boy's Moon-sign lord) is *inimical* to the girl's Moon-sign lord Jupiter. The score would be **0.**

Example : If the boy's Rasi is Leo and the girl's Rasi is Taurus, the lord of the boy's Rasi Sun is *inimical* to the girl's Moon-sign lord Venus. Likewise, the girl's Moon-sign lord Venus is also *inimical* to the boy's Moon-sign lord. The score would be **0.**

Gana

All Nakshatras are divided into 3 groups based on their nature or disposition being divine (Daivika), human (Manushya) and demonic (Rakshasa) as follows :

Daiva	Manushya	Rakshasa
Aswini	Bharani	Krittika
Mrigasira	Rohini	Aslesha
Punarvasu	Aridra	Makha
Pushya	Poorvaphalguni	Chitta
Hasta	Uttarabhadrapada	Visakha
Swati	Poorvabhadrapada	Jyeshta
Anuradha	Poorvashada	Moola
Sravana	Uttaraphalguni	Dhanishta
Revati	Uttarashada	Satabhisha

Those born under Daivika constellations are peace-loving, contented, quiet and forbearing.

Those born under Manushya stars are normally friendly and fair but under force of circumstances may be provoked to take an angry stance.

Those born under Rakshasa Nakshatra are cruel, dominating, nagging, have a tendency to inflict pain—physical, mental, emotional—and also demanding, avaricious, greedy etc.

Those belonging to the same category get along well. A Daivika constellation and Manushya star are passable. But a Daivika or a Manushya star paired with a Rakshasa star leads only to misery.

The score here is **6** points.

A Jyeshta man (Rakshasa) and a Sravana girl (Daivika) would not pair well whereas a Jyeshta man and a Krittika girl would suit each other, both being Rakshasa. Likewise, an Anuradha girl (Daivika) and Rohini (Manushya) pair would see moderate harmony.

A Daivika boy	— Daivika girl	— **6** points
A Manushya boy	— Manushya girl	— **6** points
A Rakshasa boy	— Rakshasa girl	— **6** points
A Daivika boy	— Manushya girl	— **4** points
A Daivika girl	— Manushya boy	— **4** points
A Manushya boy	— Rakshasa girl	— **2** points
A Rakshasa boy	— Manushya girl	— **2** points
A Daivika girl	— Rakshasa boy	— **0** points
A Daivika boy	— Rakshasa girl	— **0** points

Example: Boy - Jyeshta — Rakshasa
Girl - Anuradha — Daivika
Score is **0** points.

Example: Boy - Aridra — Manushya
Girl - Satabhisha— Rakshasa
Score is **2** points.

Example : Boy - Punarvasu — Daivika
Girl - Hasta — Daivika
Score is **6** points.

Rasi Kuta or Bhoo Kuta

This is dependant on the Janma Rasi or the sign where the Moon is placed. The assessment is made depending upon the mutual disposition of the Janma Rasis of the boy and the girl.

(a) If the Janma Rasi of the boy is in the 2nd from the girl's, it gives fatal results. The girl's should not be the 12th from the boy's. If the girl's is the 2nd from the boy's, it prolongs life.

Example : Boy's Janma Rasi - Aries, Girl's Janma Rasi -Taurus — long life.

Boy's Janma Rasi - Gemini, Girl's Janma Rasi - Taurus — fatal.

According to some, if the Janma Rasi of the boy is in the 2nd from the girl's and if the boy's Janma Rasi is an even sign, it bodes good and is an exception to the general rule.

If the boy's Janma Rasi is an even sign, such as Taurus, Cancer, Virgo, Scorpio, Capricorn or Pisces, then it does not matter even if it falls in the 2nd from the girl's, according to this school.

(b) If the Janma Rasi of the boy is in the 3rd from the girl's Janma Rasi, it brings misery. If the Janma Rasi of the girl is in the 3rd from the boy's, it gives happiness.

Example : If the girl's Janma Rasi is Gemini and the boy's Leo — misery. If the boy's Janma Rasi is Leo and the girl's Libra — happiness.

(c) If the boy's Janma Rasi be the 4th from the girl's,

then, it shows poverty. If the girl's is in the 4th from the boy's Janma Rasi, it gives prosperity.

Example : If the boy's Janma Rasi is Aries and the girl's Janma Rasi is Capricorn — poverty.

If the boy's Janma Rasi is Cancer and the girl's Janma Rasi is Libra — prosperity.

(d) If the boy's Janma Rasi is the 5th from the girl's, it shows widowhood. If the girl's is the 5th from the boy's Janma Rasi, it shows a long married life.

Example : If the boy's Janma Rasi is Scorpio and the girl's is Cancer — widowhood.

Example : If the boy's Janma Rasi is Sagittarius and the girl's is Aries — long married life.

(e) If the boy's Janma Rasi is the 6th from the girl's — loss of progeny. If the girl's is the 6th from the boy's, birth of children is favored.

Example : If the girl's Janma Rasi is Virgo and the boy's is Aquarius, it shows loss of progeny.

If the boy's Janma Rasi is Aquarius, and the girl's Cancer—it shows birth of children.

Where the Janma Rasi of the boy is the 6th from that of the girl, then the following exceptions are free of the adverse result, namely, loss of issue :

Aries — Virgo
Sagittarius — Taurus
Libra — Pisces
Aquarius — Cancer
Leo — Capricorn
Gemini — Scorpio

If the Janma Rasis of the boy and the girl are in diametrically opposite signs, then it conduces to a happy and long married life.

For example, if the Janma Rasis of the boy and the girl are in Cancer and Capricorn respectively, it implies happiness.

The number of units for Rasi or Bhookuta is **7**.

Nadi

All Nakshatras are divided into 3 groups coming under the 3 humours of Vata, Pitta and Kapha (Sleshma). Nakshatras coming under the same Nadi are not generally approved.

The classification is as follows:

Vata	Pitta	Sleshma
Aswini	Bharani	Krittika
Aridra	Mrigasira	Rohini
Punarvasu	Pushyami	Aslesha
Uttara	Pubba	Makha
Hasta	Chitta	Swati
Jyeshta	Anuradha	Visakha
Moola	Poorvashada	Uttarashada
Poorvabhadrapada	Uttarabhadrapada	Revati
Satabhisha	Dhanista	Sravana

The number of points given to Nadi Kuta is 8. If the two Nakshatras belong to different Nadis, the score is **8** points. Otherwise, it is **zero.**

Nadi Kuta seems to have a special reference to the health of the couple as well as of the children born to them. If other afflictions are present in the two charts and the Nadis of the boy and the girl are in the same group, it has been found that progeny born to such couples may not be healthy or even normal.

Rajju

All Nakshatras are classified into 5 groups as given in the Table.

The Nakshatras of the boy and girl should not come under the same group.

पादरज्जौ प्रवासः स्याद्रूरुरज्जौ धनक्षयः।
नाभिरज्जुः प्रजां हन्ति कण्ठरज्जुः स्त्रियं हरेत् ॥

— **Kalaprakashika,** XIII-51

Pada (feet)	Ooru (thighs)	Nabhi (navel)	Kanta (neck)	Sira (head)
Aswini	Bharani	Krittika	Rohini	Mrigasira
Aslesha	Pushya	Punarvasu	Aridra	Chitta
Makha	Purvaphalguni	Uttara-phalguni	Hasta	Dhanishta
Jyeshta	Anuradha	Visakha	Swati	—
Moola	Poorvashada	Uttarashada	Sravana	—
Revati	Uttara-bhadrapada	Poorva-bhadrapada	Satabhisha	—

If the boy and the the girl belong to the same Rajju group, the results are :

Pada — travel in distant lands
Ooru — loss or decline of wealth
Nabhi — loss of offspring
Kanta — death of wife
Sira — death of man

Rajju has not been given any numerical value, but is deemed important.

Stree Deergha

The constellation of the boy should be beyond the 9th from that of the girl in which case Stree Deergha is said to be present.

Example : Boy - Visakha
Girl - Rohini

The boy's constellation is the 13th from the girl's and therefore, Stree Deergha is said to be present.

Mahendra

The constellation of the boy should be the 4th, 7th, 10th, 12th, 16th, 19th, 22nd or the 25th from the girl's Nakshatra. The presence of Mahendra is said to support general welfare and longevity of the couple.

Example : Boy - Aridra
Girl - Krittika

The boy's constellation Aridra is the 4th from the girl's Krittika. Mahendra is present.

Exceptions

In the case of no two Nakshatras will all the factors — (a) Varna, (b) Vashya, (c) Tara, (d) Yoni, (e) Grahamaitra, (f) Gana, (g) Rasi, (h) Nadi, (i) Rajju be fulfilled.

If the lords of the Janma Rasi of the boy and the girl be the same, then the absence of Rajju, Vedha, Gana and Rasi Kutas need not be considered.

That is, for Nakshatras of the boy and the girl belonging to the following sets of Rasis, it does not matter if Rajju, Vedha, Gana and Rasi Kutas are not present :

Aries and Scorpio; Taurus and Libra; Gemini and Virgo; Sagittarius and Pisces; and Capricorn and Aquarius.

Dina, Gana, Yoni, Rasi and Rajju are the more important of the factors and if there is agreement in these, then the match can be okayed.

Agreement in Dina gives good luck; in Gana — wealth; in Mahendra—attachment; Stree Deergha — general welfare; Yoni — issues; Rasi — growth of family; Rasyadhipati (Grahamaitra) — prosperity; Vashya — cordiality, Rajju — felicity and avoidance of loss of spouse; and Vedha — many sons.

Of these several factors, at least 5 must be satisfied. Though some factors have been given a numerical rating, such rating is not conclusive. If these factors are not found satisfactory, one must also take into account omens for considering or rejecting a match.

Omens

The following are considered auspicious in negotiating a marriage proposal :

(1) A new dress; (2) flowers and fruits; (3) arrival of a couple (husband and wife); (4) someone arriving with auspicious articles *(mangaladravyas)* such as *kumkum,* turmeric, coconuts and Pooja articles as well as (5) bringing *prasadam* from some temple.

All said and done, the test of Kuta agreement must come only after the tests of longevity, mental and physical health, more than one marriage, balancing of Dosha or malefic factors and Kuja Dosha have been cleared.

The test of Kuta agrement is not decisive.

More Exceptions

The following pairs show Nakshatras that do not conduce to happiness in marriage if a boy or girl belongs to such pairs. A marriage between them is not recommended :

Krittika	-	Aslesha
Aslesha	-	Swati
Chitta	-	Poorvashada
Anuradha	-	Dhanishta
Dhanishta	-	Bharani
Satabhisha	-	Krittika

Those born under the following pairs of Nakshatras make for a happy couple :

Poorvaphalguni and Anuradha

Chitta and Pushya

Punarvasu and Hasta

Jyeshta and Satabhisha, if paired, lead to ruin of the family.

Uttaraphalguni and Mrigasira show death.

Hasta and Moola indicate financial setbacks.

Marriage between a boy and a girl coming under the following pairs are said to bestow specific results :

Many sons, if Rohini and Makha or Purvabhadrapada and Rohini.

More daughters, if Aswini and Punarvasu or Swati and Uttarashada.

Bitterness, if Revati and Aridra or Jyeshta and Uttaraphalguni.

Wicked sons, if Visakha and Makha.

Enmity between couple, if Visakha and Sravana.

Separation, if Aswini and Sravana.

Loss of spouse, if Uttarabhadrapada and Mrigasira.

Enjoyment, if Uttarashada and Revati

Prosperity, if Purvashada and Uttarabhadrapada.

Affluence, if Bharani and Pushya.

Some Exceptions

Common Nakshatra

Sometimes, it may so happen the boy and the girl may have the same Janma Nakshatra. This is generally not desirable but certain allowances are made. In fact, the same Nakṣhatra is deemed to be good in the case of the following :

Rohini, Aridra, Makha, Hasta, Visakha, Sravana, Uttarabhadrapada and Revati.

In the following cases, common Janma Nakshatra is deemed to be mediocre in results :

Aswini, Krittika, Mrigasira, Punarvasu, Pushya, Purvaphalguni, Uttaraphalguni, Chitta, Anurada, Poorvashada and Uttarashada.

Same Nakshatra and Rasi

Where the Janma Nakshatras of the boy and girl are the same, the boy's should precede the girl's.

Example : Boy — Anuradha (2)
Girl — Anuradha (4)

Since the boy's Nakshatra precedes the girl's it is not taboo.

Example : Boy — Krittika (4)
Girl — Krittika (2)

Since the girl's Nakshatra comes earlier than the boy's, it cannot be considered.

Same Rasi

Sometimes when the Janma Nakshatra is the same, it is possible the Nakshatra is limited to one sign.

Example : Boy — Makha (1)
Girl — Makha (4)

Different Rasis

But sometimes, although the Nakshatras of the boy and the girl may be the same, the signs may be different. This can happen in the case of Krittika, Mrigasira, Uttaraphalguni, Chitta, Uttarashada and Dhanishta.

In any case of common Janma Nakshatra but different signs, the girl's Nakshatra Pada should precede the boy's.

Example : Boy — Krittika (3) in Taurus
Girl — Krittika (1) in Aries

Example : Let us work out Kuta agreement between the constellation Anuradha (girl) and Jyeshta (boy).

Varna

Both constellations belong to Scorpio which comes under Brahmin and the *score* is **1** point.

Vashya

Both belong to Scorpio. Therefore, agreement is lacking. *Score:* **0** points.

Dina (Tara)

The boy's Nakshatra counted from the girl's is the 2nd. Since this figure is less than 9, it is not necessary to divide it by 9 and it is taken as remainder 2 which is good. *Score :* **3** points.

Yoni

Anuradha — female deer

Jyeshta — male deer

The Nakshatras belong to the same group and different sexes, and therefore, good. *Score :* **4** points.

Grahamaitra

Since both Nakshatras belong to Scorpio ruled by the same planet, Grahamaitra is present. *Score :* **5** points.

Gana

Girl - Daiva.

Boy - Rakshasa. *Score :* **0** points.

Rasi

The Janma Rasi of the boy and girl are in the same sign Scorpio which is good. *Score :* **7** points.

Nadi

Anuradha — Pitta

Jyeshta — Sleshma. *Score :* **8** points.

Rajju

Anuradha — Ooru (thigh)

Jyeshta — Pada (feet)

The two belonging to different Rajjus is favorable.

Therefore, the total score for this pair of Anuradha (girl) and Jyeshta (boy) works out to **28** out of **36** points which can be described as good. If Rajju is also given the numerical value of **9** points, the score would be **37/45** or 80 percent agreement in terms of *only* Kutas. This does not imply that the agreement between the charts is good, if the longevity, mental and psychological health, factors showing more than one marriage, balancing of Dosha or afflictions and Kuja Dosha factors have not been evaluated. ●

Chapter VII

The Sun Dasa and Marital Disasters

VII

The Sun is the central point around which the whole concept of astrology revolves. The Sun is variously known as *Grahapurusha* or sustainer of the Grahas, *Rajyakaraka* or significator of political power and *Pitrukaraka* or significator of the father. His position in the chart assumes great importance in assessing the foundational strength of the chart. The Sun is extolled as predominantly good natured or Sattwic, *vide* **Jataka Parijata** II -543.

प्रतापशाली चतुरस्त्रदेहः
श्यामारुणाङ्गो मधुपिङ्गलाक्षः।
पित्तात्मकः स्वल्पकचाभिरामो
दिवाकरः सत्वगुणप्रधानः ॥

meaning, *possessed of energy, of square build, dark-red streaked yellowish eyes, intoxicated looking (egoistic ?), of a Pitta-constitution, with sparse hair, the Sun is Sattwagunapradhanah or predominantly Sattwic-natured.*

The Sun is described as *Kalatma* or representing the soul. Basically, as the Karaka for the 9th and 10th houses, he is said to govern ultimate knowledge and truth. In fact, this is brought out in the *Gayatri Mantra* which is addressed to the Sun as *Savitr* seeking enlightenment and knowledge.

Results attributed to the Sun in various houses are usually favorable and these manifest in his Dasa. Most of the classical works give similar results for the Sun in the different houses with some minor variations in between. For example, *the Sun in the Ascendant* is said to give thinning hair, a life of ease, few sons, defective vision, make one well-bred and regal in bearing. *If afflicted,* one becomes conceited. *If well-placed,* it conduces to acquisition of *Gnana* or Ultimate Knowledge, health, good vision and other benefic results. *In the second,* it makes one liberal, possess much property in minerals, eloquent but with wicked desires. *In the 3rd,* the Sun makes one brave, with treacherous servants, very wealthy and liberal. The Sun is not in a very happy position *in the 4th,* for then, one becomes hard-pressed for money, suffers from heart-conditions, lacks in resources and common-sense, and becomes hard-hearted. *The Sun in the 5th* gives one clout in government circles. It makes one of unsteady mind and always travelling. One becomes lustful, brave, honoured by kings, full of self-esteem, renowned and rich with *the Sun in the 6th. When the Sun is in the 7th Bhava,* one hates women and is exceedingly fierce and wrathful. Winning ways, discontent and being good at arguments are attributed to *the Sun in the 8th.* One becomes a heretic, hates his parents, religion and spiritual teacher and converts to another religion with the *Sun occupying the 9th house. In the 10th* where he gets Digbala, the Sun bestows on one wealth by inheritance, virtue, fame, success and status. *The 11th* is also a good place for the Sun to occupy, for then, he confers extensive wealth, wife, children, retinue and happiness while *in the 12th,* although he makes one energetic, it leads to physical defect or deformity, apostasy and vagrancy.

The results are of a varied nature but do not seem to touch any matters connected with marital life except, perhaps, when in the 7th when it makes one a *Stree-dweshi* or hate women. Such a situation naturally blights marital life, for, no one who hates women, generally can love his own wife. In a female chart, it creates a like situation where the native is filled with bitterness and anger for the husband. This is where some confusion enters the picture. Malefics, it is well-known, in the 2nd, 4th, 7th, 8th and 12th houses ruling family, domestic happiness, spouse, longevity of marriage and conjugal life respectively are said to spoil marital happiness for one reason or the other. And by malefics, we usually mean Mars, Saturn, Rahu and Ketu. Afflicted Mercury and a weak Moon are also classed as malefics. The Sun as the embodiment of Ultimate Knowledge is generally not described as malefic. Nor is he, inspite of being Sattwic, considered a benefic. In some texts, the Sun is called a *Krura* or cruel planet. He is fiery in nature, bilious in temperament and blazing. These attributes are common to Mars who is also said to be hot in nature, bilious and wrathful. And Mars, as we know, has the dubious distinction of creating havoc in married life. In fact,

धनवसानस्मरयानरन्ध्रगो धरासुतोजन्मनि यस्य दारहा ।
तथैव कन्याजन जन्मलग्नतौ यदि क्षमासूनुरनिषदः पतेः ॥

— **Jataka Parijata,** XIV-34

Mars occupying the 2nd, 12th, 7th, 4th or the 8th in the horoscope of a person may cause the death of the wife. If Mars occupies these same

positions in the horoscope of a woman, it proves injurious to the husband. Such a disposition of Mars may result either in death or estrangement between the couple leading to mutual acrimony and hate.

Results of the Sun occupying the 2nd, 4th, 7th, 8th or 12th house in a chart, more or less, follow the same pattern as of Mars occupying these Bhavas. Perhaps, the difference lies in the fact that when the Sun gives these results, the native begins to look inwards for peace and thus embarks on the journey to Ultimate Knowledge. No matter, it may be slow or barely preceptible. But the orientation of the psyche undergoes a distinct transformation and the native begins to engage in a process of spiritual searching and inquiry. This is where the Sun's Sattwa Guna shows up. Sattwa Guna is usually translated as "good nature" in most astrological texts. But this is rather inadequate and does not do justice to the term. Sattwa may be understood as that which ennobles one and uplifts the soul. The pain and trauma of the marital disaster give a feeling of revulsion for the grosser things of life and the native, for the first time, may be, in this life, begins to get the feeling that life is more than external relationships and mundane pursuits. One may still continue in all of life's activities which one was earlier involved in; only now, the Sun has stirred a relatively unknown corner of one's being and set into motion a process of de-attachment and disentanglement. The pace of this process may not even be felt or sensed but it has begun, marking the first step towards the upward evolution of the soul in this particular embodiment, taking off perhaps from the stage at which the process had come to a halt in an earlier state of existence.

Mars, on the other hand, when he destroys or damages marital life, creates strong reactions of resentment, revenge and frustration so that the native engages in a pattern of thought that is ruled and dictated by these disintegrative emotions. Such a motivation may lead one to renewed efforts to regain what has been lost or even to gain something better than before, but only on a gross level. Mars does not allow one to accept the loss forcing the native again into a whirl of pursuit of similar objectives like the moth which is attracted by the burning flame only to be reduced to ashes by it. With the Sun, the pain, the disappointment, the disillusionment and anger following the marital disaster are very much there; but the direction of the reaction is ennobling and uplifting of the soul. As Atmakaraka, the Sun's primary concern is not rehabilitation of the native's shattered mundane activities and pursuits but re-orientation of the soul, caught in the dualities of life towards a freedom that is possible only when one steps beyond these dualities. Irrespective of the lordship of the Sun, these changes occur in the individual at varying degrees and levels determined by the general potential of the chart for spiritual growth.

Let us move on to the more tangible part of the results the Sun can give. Another difference between the Sun and Mars in these houses is that the results begin to manifest in Sun Dasa or just before it is due to start, that is, in the previous Dasa of Venus in the last two Bhuktis of Mercury and Ketu particularly. In the case of Mars, it is not necessarily confined to or tagged to Mars Dasa. The blow to the marriage can come in any other Dasa too, so long as it is of a planet related to or afflicting houses connected with domestic happiness.

Chart 17: Born 3-5-1962 at 7-15 a.m. at 13N 08, 80 E 18 with a balance of 4 years, 4 months and 21 days of Ketu Dasa at birth.

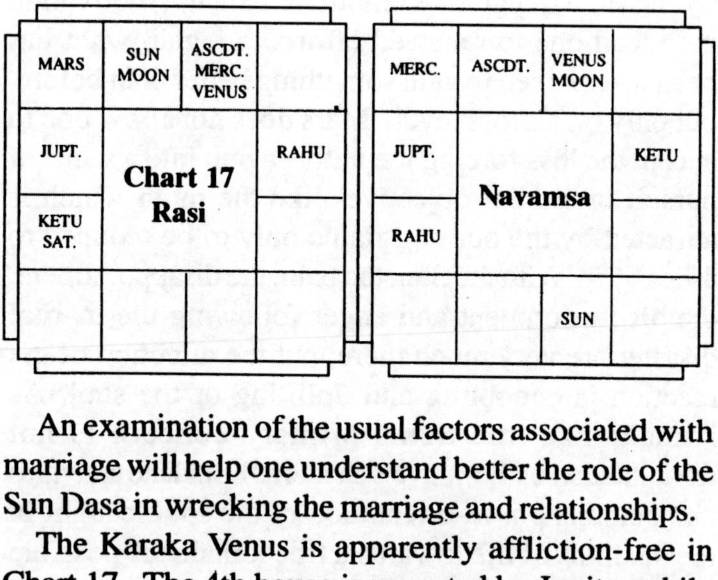

An examination of the usual factors associated with marriage will help one understand better the role of the Sun Dasa in wrecking the marriage and relationships.

The Karaka Venus is apparently affliction-free in Chart 17. The 4th house is aspected by Jupiter while the 4th lord Sun, even if in exaltation, occupies the 12th. The 8th house is affliction-free, so also the 7th. The 7th lord is in the 11th which *per se* is not an affliction. The 12th house is quite heavily afflicted by the New Moon. With reference to the Moon-sign, the Moon as the 4th lord ruling domestic happiness lacks Pakshabala. Rahu occupies the 4th house. Mars and Saturn aspect the 7th house. These factors afflict the chart in terms of marital life.

The facts of the case: The native, a young girl, fell in love with a young man and the two, fearing parental opposition, went in for a civil marriage. However, the parents of both got to know of it. The boy's parents were vehemently, even hysterically, against it. The girl's parents were more realistic and accepted their daughter's marriage, even if they did not welcome it. The marriage was registered on 13-1-1984. The girl met her husband for the last time on 20-11-1984, although at that time she did not know it. On 21-11-1984, the boy's parents packed him off abroad promising him his wife would follow him shortly. But once the boy was gone, his parents refused to have anything to do with the girl. They did not even give her an inkling of his destination. The girl's parents tried to locate him but could not trace him and she never saw or heard from him again.

The boy and the girl met in October 1982 and fell in love in Mercury Bhukti of Venus Dasa. The marriage and the separation took place in this period. Unfortunately, she was moving into Ketu Bhukti which marks the concluding part of Venus Dasa. The Dasa due to start next was of the Sun who afflicts the 12th house. As 4th lord in the 12th, he ruined her personal life. With reference to the Moon-sign, the Sun afflicts the 4th lord Moon by his proximity destroying Sukastana — all happiness. Additionally, but not by itself, the transit of Saturn in the 7th and the 8th from the natal Moon opened up the chart to the danger inherent in the Dasa lord.

Venus, the Kalatrakaraka, is not only in his own sign but also Vargottama. Yet, the fact he occupies Rohini ruled by the New Moon in the 12th house overcame the other positive features of Venus, depriving the girl of marital happiness.

Mars can kill the spouse; the Sun does not kill but wrenches the couple apart bringing in more pain and anguish than Mars can generate.

Chart 18: Born 13-10-1954 at 4-10 a.m. at 13 N 10, 78 E 10 with a balance of 3 years, 0 months and 1 day of Ketu Dasa at birth.

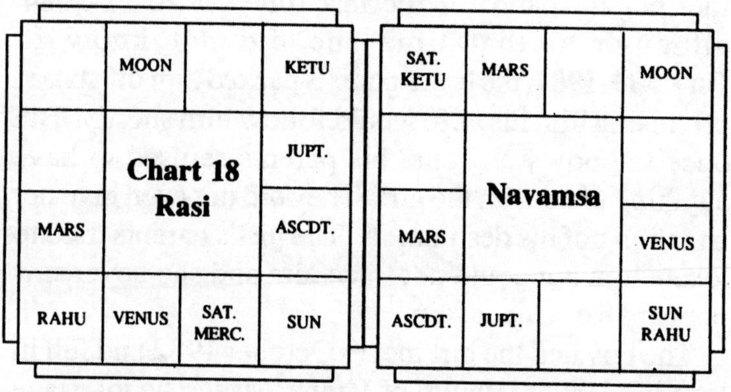

The afflictions in Chart 18 are not so obvious but what is cause for concern is the Sun in the 2nd house. Venus in the 4th is not bad and is even aspected by exalted Jupiter. The 7th lord Saturn is exalted and with 2nd and 11th lord Mercury which does not conduce to good results. From Chandra Lagna too, the 7th house has Mercury and exalted 11th lord Saturn. This Mercury-Saturn combine acting on the 7th house gave the native an unfaithful husband. The native got married in June 1974 to a man who had been having an affair for many years before that. The native did her best to wean him away from his mistress. When he bluntly refused to leave her preferring her to his legally wedded wife, the latter left him in sheer disgust in October 1978.

As in the previous case, the marriage came in Venus Dasa, Mercury Bhukti. The sordid affair came to light soon after so that the native really was never happy in her marriage. The divorce came in Sun Dasa. The Sun is the Lagna lord in the 2nd house but did nothing to save the marital interests of the native.

Chart 19: Born 18-5-1966 at 10-30 p.m. (IST) at 13 N, 77 E 35 with a balance of 2 years, 5 months and 15 days of Ketu Dasa at birth.

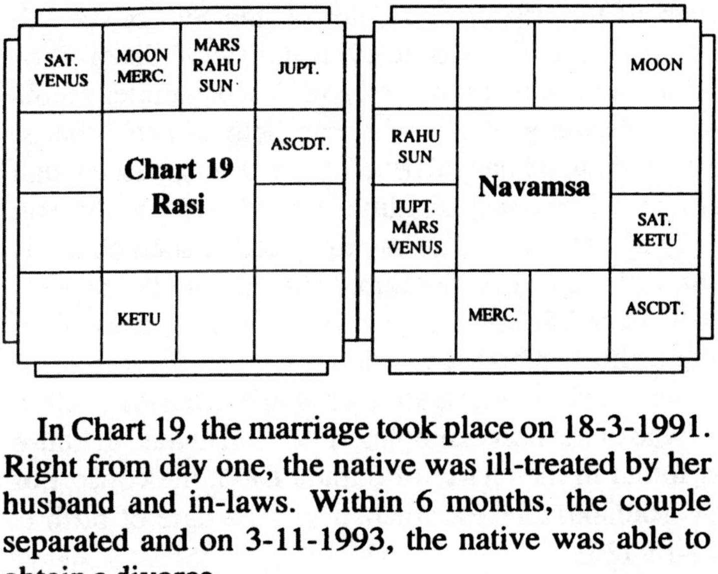

In Chart 19, the marriage took place on 18-3-1991. Right from day one, the native was ill-treated by her husband and in-laws. Within 6 months, the couple separated and on 3-11-1993, the native was able to obtain a divorce.

The afflictions in Chart 19 are not very obvious. The 7th lord Saturn in a common sign with the Karaka Venus also there can, but not necessarily, indicate more than one marriage. The Sun as the 2nd lord is in the

11th from Lagna joined by explosive Mars and incendiary Rahu. He is aspected by Saturn. With reference to the Moon-sign, the Sun occupies the 2nd house in heavy affliction. All the unhappiness and the divorce were gone through in Sun Dasa.

Such charts show, with unfalling regularity, the maleficence inbuilt into the Dasa of the Sun placed in the 2nd, 4th, 7th, 8th or 12th houses either from the Lagna or the Moon-sign. In such charts, marriage taking place in the closing years of Venus Dasa or in the Sun Dasa, stands exposed to the danger of breaking up in the latter Dasa, unless there is a strong relieving factor such as the aspect of Jupiter on the Sun or the 7th house when the worst eventuality of divorce or permanent spearation can be diffused. Jupiter seems to be the only planet who can help in such charts. Venus, though a natural benefic, can never get far enough from the Sun to aspect him. His proximity to the Sun only afflicts him. The saving grace in such charts is Jupiter's aspect on the Sun. The 5th and 9th aspects help. The 7th house aspect rarely does because then Jupiter himself becomes Vakra or retrograde when some of the genial qualities associated with him fail to manifest.

One of the best examples of the Sun in the 7th house is found in the chart* of Sarada Devi, the consort of Sri Ramakrishna Paramahamsa. The date of birth is 22-12-1853.

The Sun in Chart 20 is in the 7th house with the 7th lord Jupiter. There are other afflictions too but our

---

*Courtesy: *Sri Sarada Devi—The Holy Mother* by Swami Tapasyananda, page 374.

focus is on the Sun in the 7th house. The husband was a highly illumined soul who became a beacon light to thousands of spiritual seekers. Blazing with spiritual lustre like the Sun himself, Sri Ramakrishna Paramahamsa never led married life in the conventional sense of the term. That Sarada Devi was uncomplaining, being herself a rare soul of great spiritual attainments, is another matter. But honestly, would any parent be

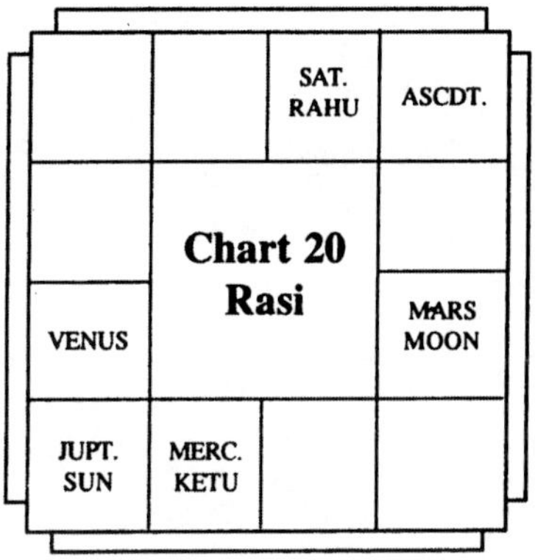

Chart 20
Rasi

happy with the kind of conjugal life Chart 20 shows for one's own son or daughter ?

The Sun is basically a spiritual planet and many times, it is his Dasa that triggers metaphysical questions in one's heart. Naturally, his position in Bhavas governing marital matters and domestic relationships cannot conduce to warmth and cordiality. Rather, the results he gives are such as to bring in disillusionment in these areas of life so that the truth of all relationships as being ephemereal and fleeting is brought into sharp focus preparing the ground for the native to realign his sights on the purpose of human birth and the evolution of his soul. ●

Chapter VIII

Detecting Dowry Dangers

The abnoxious practice of demanding dowry at a marriage has gathered force in recent times. More and more cases of dowry are coming to light. While such cases highlight the plight and misery of young brides, they also are a sad commentary on the decline in moral values in the social system. No fair thinking individual will endorse this unhealthy social practice which thrives on greed, avarice and exploitation. That this system centres on marriage is in itself a big shock and an index to the levels to which human sensitivity, rather insensitivity, can dip.

Marriage was, and still is, considered a sacrament in Hindu society. It has, however, its social, religious as well as legal aspects. The primary object of this institution is to provide a stable and sound unit for society to develop around. While in some countries, the individual is the smallest unit of the social order to which he belongs, in India barring a minuscule percentage, it is the family. Not only does this unit ensure the cultural roots of the individual but also provides a broad framework within which his aspirations and urges can take constructive shape without abnormal suppression or licentious promiscuousness.

There is no question of receiving gifts, in cash or kind, as a matter of right by either party, in the concept of marriage if properly interpreted according to scriptural injunctions. The marriage solemnisation binds the couple to remain faithful to each other and never seek to desert each other for reasons of righteousness

(Dharma), money (Artha) or gratification of desire and pursuit of pleasure (Kama). The bond is held so sacred that it cannot be questioned or discarded for any of these reasons. But should either of the parties seek release from the marital bond for the specific reason of Ultimate Enlightenment or Moksha, the sacrament does allow release.

This is how marriage is envisaged in the scriptures. Most Indians still abide by this definition, and in doing so, grow in moral and spiritual evolution, learning to bear each other's shortcomings, remaining faithful to each other and looking upon any calamity to the other as one common to both. In this exercise and endeavour to abide by the spirit of the union, the couple, more often than not, grows in patience, forbearance, compassion and also self-denial. It was for the fostering of these qualities that marriage was orginally intended. Birth after birth as the individual advanced in his soul evolution, even without his being aware of it, he was gradually, but surely, being directed towards the Ultimate Goal of Sanatana Dharma — Moksha.

But with modernisation and industrialization taking over the country and with formal education producing more and more literates, somehow, soul-culture got lost on the way. The way people began to look at marriage, the money angle began to assume undue prominence. Everything was spoken of as a money proposition. Dowry became an essential and integral ingredient of marriage in many families that had drifted afar from the cultural and moral values enshrined in Sanatana Dharma. Such families were traditional in food, dress and other outward forms of life-style. Only the pivot of their existence had shifted from Dharma to Artha.

Dowry, in the ultimate analysis, is another word for socially legitimatized greed. The dowry demand begins with the first stage of the marital process, when the boy's and girl's families meet to consider and negotiate the alliance. In some cases, it seeps in after the marriage. It starts with the harassment of the bride by the husband and his family for not bringing in gifts or money. How much is defined only by the avarice index of the groom and his family. This ill-treatment of the young woman may take on different forms—humiliation, coldness, harsh words, mental, and sometimes, even physical cruelty. Many women's organisations clamouring for women's liberation and female emancipation must not, in their excitement, overlook the fact that it is not harassment of the weaker sex by only the male but also members of their own sex.

In cases of dowry, the entire marital home develops or reeks of a sick atmosphere. It is hard to find cases where the husband alone acts thus and the rest of his family sympathises with the young wife. Therefore, apart from the 7th and 8th houses, the 4th house becomes a very important factor in identifying dowry-prone charts.

In one case (Chart 21), the girl who got married on 23-6-1991 was harassed for money, right from the same day. Unable to bear the cruelty, she returned home and applied for divorce.

The 7th lord Venus is heavily afflicted by Saturn, Ketu, Rahu and Mars. The 8th lord Mercury in the 4th is aspected by Mars (Neecha and with Rahu). The 4th lord Saturn also suffers affliction vitiating the marital home atmosphere. Considered from the Moon, the 2nd lord Venus is blemished by being with Saturn-Ketu and

Chart 21: Born 11-3-1963 at 11-10 a.m. (IST) at 14 N 42, 77 E 05 with a balance of 7 years, 10 months and 15 days of Moon Dasa.

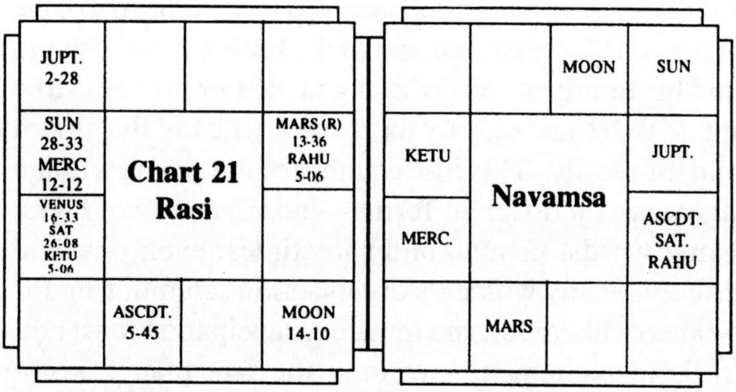

aspected by Mars-Rahu. The 8th lord Mars is himself badly placed showing the high-voltage tension and torment the girl had to face in her marital home.

The Dasa was of Rahu upto February 1996. Rahu contaminates the 7th, 2nd and 4th lords and is himself afflicted by them. Thereafter, begins Jupiter Dasa with Jupiter better placed. Therefore, the girl's life could normalise with Jupiter Dasa but not before she gets her divorce in Rahu Dasa.

In yet another case (Chart 22), the young woman wrote "Today is my third wedding anniversary..... but life has been miserable..... yet I want to live". This girl had agreed to marry in the first place becasue there was no demand for dowry either *before* or *at* the marriage. But some days after the marriage, the husband's family began humiliating and ill-treating her because she had not brought in any dowry with her.

Chart 22: Born 26-8-1949 at 5-48 p.m. (IST) at 26 N 55, 80 E 59 with a balance of 7 years, 0 months and 22 days of Moon Dasa.

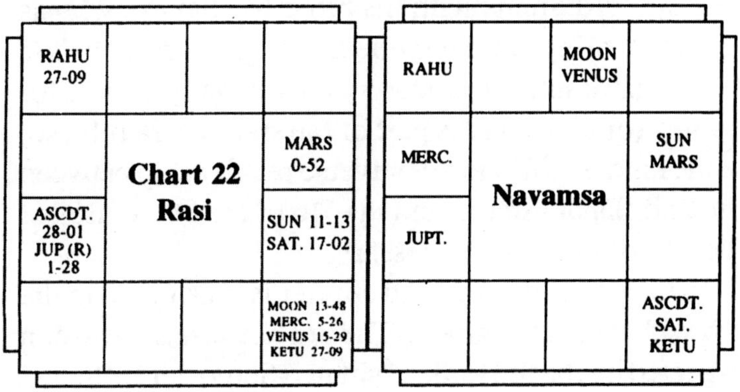

Most surprisingly, it was the husband who would say unpleasant things and later, the entire family would get together calling her names, and finally, after only 3 months and 20 days of staying together, she was disowned by the husband and his family.

Marriage took place as soon as Jupiter Dasa began. The 7th house shows the husband and the 2nd from the 7th, namely, the 8th house, his family. The 7th house is occupied by Neecha or debilitated Mars while the 7th lord Moon is in the 9th in Virgo with Venus and Mercury-cum-Ketu. Further, retrograde Jupiter aspects the whole lot. The husband should have been a friendly gentle-natured man since the 7th lord Moon is well-placed. But a look at the chart from the Moon-sign changes the whole picture. Not only is the

7th lord Jupiter retrograde or Vakra making the husband perverse but because he is aspected by the worst malefic Mars (3rd and 8th lord), also extremely selfish and vicious-natured.

The 8th house from Lagna has a combust Saturn. The 8th lord Sun is with his bitter foe Saturn, who as 2nd lord, brings in the monetary angle as responsible for the girl's suffering. Dowry is essentially avarice for money (or kind) on the part of the spouse's family; so, some kind of affliction or adverse relationship between the 2nd (Dhanastana) and the 7th or the 8th houses or their lords becomes necessary.

In Chart 23, the 7th lord Jupiter is retrograde in the 4th with Ketu retrograde. The 8th house has the Moon aspected by the 8th lord debilitated Saturn and afflicted

Chart 23: Born 11-4-1969 at 10-30 a.m. at 15 N 51, 78 E 01.

RAHU 7-19 SUN 29-10 VENUS 25-0	MERC. 1-39 SAT. 5-39		ASCDT. 7-24
	Chart 23		
MOON 20-25	**Rasi**		
	MARS 23-15		JUPT. 6-39 KETU 7-19

SUN	MERC.	SAT.	
KETU VENUS JUPT.	**Navamsa**		
MARS			RAHU
ASCDT.			

7th lord Jupiter. The Moon, incidentally, is the 2nd lord, showing Dhana or money.

The 4th house has the aspect of a Rahu-afflicted Karaka Venus and the Sun. The girl who had a good job before marriage was forced to give it up. Her in-laws and spouse began to ill-treat her demanding that she get gold and money from her parents. She continues to live in her in-laws' place. The Dasa is of Rahu who afflicts the 4th house, the 7th lord Jupiter as also Kalatrakaraka Venus.

The final outcome of a dowry case is determined by the Dasa-Bhuktis and inherent strength of the girl's horoscope.

An Alpayu chart with serious afflictions to the 7th and 8th houses can be described as a potential dowry death case. Mars and Rahu would be more malefic in such cases than Saturn, since inhuman cruelty characterises such tragedies.

The marriage of another unhappy victim (Chart 24) who was not lucky as the other two cases, occurred on 30-6-1975 in Ketu Bhukti of Mars Dasa.

Chart 24: Born 19-10-1959 at 11-45 p.m. (IST) at 20 N 56, 77 E 48.

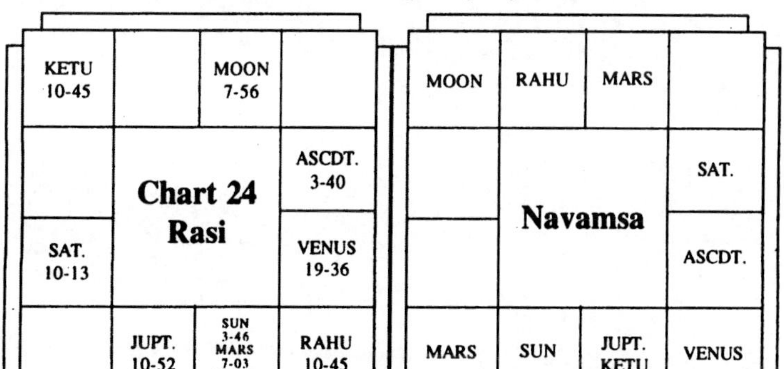

Malefics occupy Kendras. No benefics are in angles. The 8th lord Saturn is in the 12th therefrom.

The 7th lord (who is also the 8th lord here) is aspected by combust Mars. The 4th house has a combust Mars aspected by 7th and 8th lord Saturn. On 2-7-1975, barely 2 days after she got married, the girl died in a fire in her in-laws' house. No information, as to how the fire started, was available and the girl's parents were left only with a charred body.

When there are indications for marital cruelty, the best solution is to wait for the adverse Dasa to finish. This may not always be practical. At such times, the girl should also be trained for a job and career. Where marriage is a sacrament, the bond must be respected and preserved even in the face of heavy odds. But where one party to a marriage treats it as a money-producing institution, the aggrieved party should be geared to walk out of it and fend for herself. ●

Chapter IX

Watching out for Loss of Spouse

IX

Widowhood is one of the most catastrophic calamities in the life of a woman, especially when it strikes in the early years of marriage. Loss of spouse for men can be devastating too but given the social, economic and psychological factors involved in such a situation, it is the woman whose life is hurt more deeply by such an event.

That is why perhaps, the subject of marriage and its duration receives particular attention in almost all classical works of astrology. Where marriage was deemed to be the be all and end all of a woman's life, its course, quality and span could never be treated with scant regard in an astrological understanding of a chart. The modern young woman may not quite agree with this line of thinking. Modern-day attitudes precede from a shallow vision of life, lacking in foresight and the maturity that comes of the wisdom of generations. Career goals, money, foreign jaunts, interests — mental, intellectual, artistic and other — and socialising seem to be all important and marriage, with so much excitement around, is deemed an unwanted intrusion. But one must note that time never stands still—yesterday has become today and today will soon be relegated to the past with tomorrow taking over, but even that only temporarily. For, tomorrow must soon slide back into the past. The twenties and thirties are an age of exuberance, energy and zest and one can justifiably feel on top of the world. But pray, for how long ? Age creeps in from behind pushing one all too soon into middle age and then, old age when the charms of youth begin to fade and cease to be relevant. It is at such a stage in life that one may be forced to realise that marriage, not only for its own sake, but also as an insurance for the travails of middle and old age, is a necessary institution.

Probably, such logic has been behind the importance given to assessing the merits of marriage in a woman's chart for, after all she is more vulnerable than man, whether in India or abroad. One may point out cases of women who have led single lives as being happy but this is only a superficial assessment in 99 percent of the cases. Open up their hearts and you will find that they are bitter, angry, cynical and lonely, inspite of male or female companionship outside of marriage. Marriage gives mellowness to both the body and mind, and therefore, after a certain stage in one's life, even if one is deprived of one's spouse, one is better geared to carry on than one who has never married.

A British poet wrote "It is better to have loved and lost, than not have loved at all". Let me paraphrase on that — It is better to have married and lost (the spouse), than not have married at all. So much for why widowhood is given importance in a female chart.

A knowledge that a chart holds indications for loss of spouse helps one plan one's life better. It also helps in choosing the right chart for a marital alliance, rejecting those that can aggravate the indications and choosing that which can diffuse the indication.

Widowhood (including loss of wife) generally strikes

when least expected. Like death, many charts are deceptively misleading when it comes to identifying loss of spouse by death. Classical texts carry many combinations for such a tragedy. Some of these combinations work literally; others have to be suitably adapted. I must caution readers at this stage that a fatalistic interpretation of the chart should not be given. Astrology is indicative, not deterministic.

Some combinations commonly found in almost all classical works for loss of husband (or wife) are given below :

(a) The lords of the 7th and 8th houses together and occupying the 8th house aspected by malefic planets.

For example, if for a Scorpio Ascendant, if Venus and Mercury occupy Gemini and are aspected by Saturn, it can show widowhood.

(b) Rahu in the 7th, the 7th lord conjoining the Sun aspected by the 8th lord.

(c) Mars in the 8th with the 8th lord and Lagna in malefic Navamsa.

(d) Rahu joined by Mars and Saturn in the 7th or 8th can show early widowhood.

(e) If the 7th lord is malefic and Mars and Saturn are in the 7th or the 8th.

(f) If the 7th and its lord are between malefics in conjunction with no benefics or not aspected by benefics.

(g) If the Navamsa lord of the 7th is in debility, eclipsed or combust or between evil planets and unfavorable Shadvargas.

According to **Brihat Parasara Hora,** the Moon in

Cancer in Saturn's Trimsamsa can also show widowhood.

If Mars occupies the 7th, widowhood comes very soon after marriage.

Malefics in the 7th also show widowhood.

Mars in the 8th is treated with dread.

कुजेऽष्टमगते बाला कृशांगी रोगसंयुता ।
विधवा कान्तिहीना च शोकसन्तापदुःखिता ।

— Chap. 82-28

The female native with Mars in the 8th is endowed with a weak physique, is sickly, will be struck by widowhood, is not beautiful and will face destitution and distress.

The most commonly known combinations for widowhood are dominated by the positions of Mars.

लग्ने व्यये सुखे वाऽपि सप्तमे वाऽष्टमे कुजे ।
शुभदृग्योगहीने च पतिं हन्ति न संशयः ॥

— Part II, Chap. 82, Sl. 47

*If Mars, **bereft of the aspect or conjunction of an auspicious (or benefic) planet** is posited in the Ascendant, the 12th, the 4th, the 7th or the 8th, the husband of such a person will certainly meet with early death.*

These Yogas are not absolute and should not be taken as decisive because the next two Slokas make provision for relief from such Martian dispositions.

यस्मिन् योगे समुत्पन्ना पतिं हन्ति कुमारिका ।
तस्मिन् योगे समुत्पन्नो पत्नीं हन्ति नरोपि च ॥
स्त्रीहन्त्रा परिणीता चेत् पतिहन्त्री कुमारिका ।
तदा वैधव्ययोगस्य भंगो भवति निश्चयात् ॥

— Chap. 82-48, 49

If a man takes birth under a Yoga, similar to the Yoga in which a woman takes birth and attains widowhood, he will become a widower. If a woman with such a Yoga marries a man with a similar Yoga, it will cause cancellation of such a Yoga.

In another version of the **Brihat Parasara Hora** it says, under *Strijatakaphaladhyayah,*

पत्युः कलत्रतो रन्ध्राद् वैधव्यस्य द्विजोत्तम ।
असंगतं कलत्रेषु पत्यौ तत्फलमीरयेत् ॥

— Chap. 80-4

From the 7th house, the husband; from the 8th, widowhood are to be examined. (Yogas) that cannot be applied to women must be applied to their husbands.

Under *Patighatakayoga* (Yoga for destruction of husband), the same edition says,

पातालेऽपि तनौ रन्ध्रे जामित्रे वापि च व्यये ।
स्थितः कुजः पतिं हन्ति न चेच्छुभयुतेक्षितः ॥

— Chap. 80-48

If Mars bereft of the aspect or association of benefics be in 1, 4, 7, 8, 12, the husband dies.

इन्दोरप्युक्तगेहेषु स्थितो भौमोऽथवा शनिः ।
पतिहन्ता स्त्रियाश्चैवं वरस्य यदि स्त्रीमृतिः ॥

— Chap. 80-49.

If Mars or Saturn occupy these houses from the Moon-sign, then also the native's husband dies. If such planetary dispositions occur in a man's chart, then his wife dies.

The next Sloka on *Vaidhavyayogabhanga* deals with the **cancellation of the Yoga for widowhood.**

स्त्रीणां वैधव्यदो योगः पुंसां जन्मनि चेद् भवेत् ।
तदा पत्नीविनाशः स्या-दुभयोश्चेच्छुभं स्मृतम् ॥

— Chap. 80-50

If the combinations for widowhood in a woman's chart obtain in a man's chart, it leads to destruction (death) of wife. However, if present in the charts of both the man and the woman, it causes good (auspiciousness) to both.

Therefore, although dealt with under *Streejataka* in most classical works, combinations for widowhood are equally effective in bringing about **death of wife** in male charts. These combinations, it must be noted, are not absolute and can be remedied by matching charts with similarity in afflicting factors.

Mars occupies the 8th house in Chart 25 while Saturn is in the 2nd. Saturn is aspected by Jupiter. Mars, on the contrary, gets further afflicted by Saturn's aspect. The native lost her husband when she was 48 years old in tragic circumstances.

Chart 25: Born 23-3-1929 at 10-51 a.m. (IST) at 18 N 56, 72 E 51 with a balance of 8 years, 0 months and 18 days of Venus Dasa at birth.

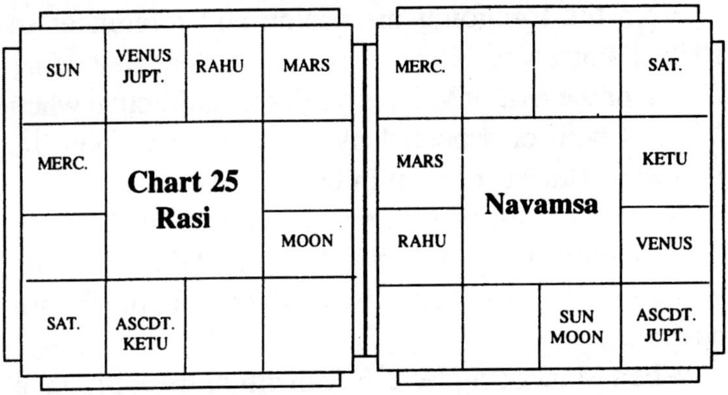

Two conditions, each individually capable of decimating the spouse, are present in Chart 26. Saturn in Lagna is also deemed to be a spouse killer coming

Chart 26: Born 9-12-1946 at 9-30 p.m. (ZST) at 45 N 30, 11 E 33.

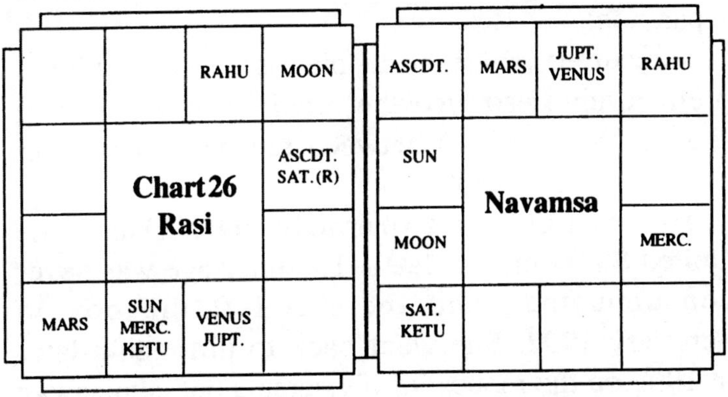

under the Yoga that requires either Mars or Saturn in the 1st, 2nd, 4th, 7th, 8th or 12th from Lagna or the Moon. Mars in the 7th from the Moon is also a serious affliction showing widowhood. The native's husband died when she was 45 years old, also in tragic circumstances.

From the foregoing discussion and references to **Brihat Parasara Hora,** it becomes clear that *Mars Dosha* or the *Evil of Mars* is rendered ineffective when Mars is with or aspected by benefics and when the *Dosha of Mars* is present in both charts.

A careful study of several charts with these combinations has, however, shown that there is some variance in the results attributed to Mars in the fateful positions.

When Mars occupies the 2nd, 4th or the 12th, then it leads to friction and bickering and bitterness between spouses but rarely to death of spouse.

When Mars occupies the 7th, in most cases it has not killed the spouse but estranged the couple bringing in deep hatred for each other that has even led to separation.

Sometimes, where the couple has been happy, it has prematurely destroyed the relationship by forcing separation (physical) between the two for reasons beyond one's control.

The native of Chart 27 married a boy working in the United States on 1-9-1991. The marriage was never consummated and the girl left the boy in February 1992. She went back to him again later in 1992 on the request of his parents but came away after 14 days on 25-8-1992. A divorce was obtained in February 1994.

Mars occupies the 7th from the Ascendant and is rendered extremely malefic by his retrogression.

Chart 27: Born 1-7-1969 at 4-00 a.m. (IST) at 25 N 20, 83 E 00 with a balance of 3 years, 3 months and 11 days of Sun Dasa at birth.

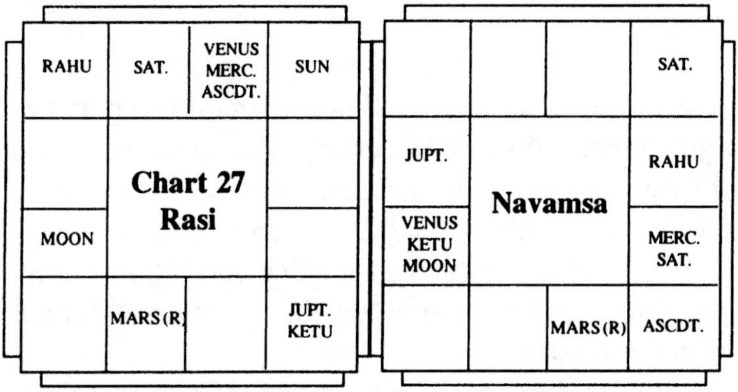

A closer look at the chart shows Saturn in the 12th from the Lagna and in the 4th from the Moon. Mars(R) occupies the 7th from Venus, the Kalatrakaraka, as well.

Therefore, when Mars blasts a marital relationship, the affliction can come out not only when he occupies the 7th from Lagna or the Moon but even from the Kalatrakaraka Venus.

When Mars is in the 2nd, he would aspect the 8th house or Mangalyastana and bring it under stress. When in the 7th itself, he not only damages the 7th but also the 2nd house by his aspect.

Mars in the 1st house afflicts the 7th and 8th houses.

In the 8th, as Mangalyakaraka in the 8th, he is anything but welcome.

In all these instances, only the 7th and 8th house aspects have been taken into account, but even considering the 4th house aspect of Mars, it extends to one or more of these sensitive houses irrespective of which of the 1st, 2nd, 4th, 7th, 8th or 12th houses he occupies.

Mars in these houses is deemed to destroy marital happiness, but if associated or aspected by a benefic, it gets toned down considerably. For example, Mars and Venus in the 7th for an Aquarius Ascendant native left his spouse untouched. In yet another case, Mars, Saturn and Rahu in the 8th for a Scorpio Moon-Lagna with Jupiter in Libra aspecting the malefic trio did not harm the spouse.

Likewise, Mars as a Yogakaraka for Cancer and Leo natives may be said to be generally harmless.

Chart 28 : Born 21-4-1926 at 2-40 a.m. at 51 N 32, 00 W 05 with a balance of 11 years, 9 months and 25 days of Mercury Dasa at birth.

MERC.	SUN		RAHU
JUPT. VENUS	Chart 28 Rasi		MOON
MARS ASCDT.			
KETU	SAT. (R)	MANDI	

	VENUS		SUN RAHU
MANDI	Navamsa		SAT.
MOON ASCDT.			
KETU		MERC.	MARS

In Queen Elizabeth's case (Chart 28), Mars occupies the 7th from the Moon giving rise to an affliction from Mars for **loss of spouse.** But, as Mars is a functional benefic for the Moon-sign Cancer, it ceases to be effective.

However, if other afflictions are present, then the spouse may die early.

Chart 29 is an excellent illustration of the havoc Mars may cause when in the 8th house if supported by other afflictions, irrespective of his being a Yogakaraka or not.

Chart 29 : Born 19-11-1917 at 11-13 p.m. (IST) at 25 N 27, 81 E 51 with a balance of 1 year, 3 months and 25 days of Sun Dasa at birth.

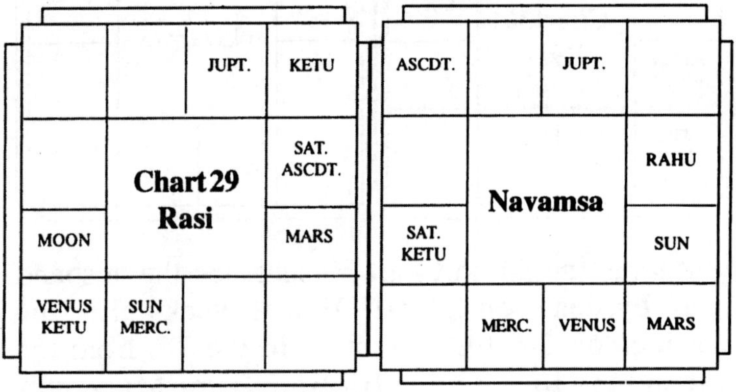

There is Mars in the 8th from the Moon-sign. Malefic Saturn occupies the Lagna, also unfavorable for protecting the spouse. The native lost her husband about 16 years after marriage. But even when he was alive, they were estranged and lived apart.

Likewise, for an Aries Ascendant with Mars in the 8th in Scorpio, inspite of being a functional benefic as Lagna Lord, he did nothing to protect the spouse. The native lost her husband in her early twenties. However, as the 8th lord in the 8th, he made sure she lived beyond 80 years.

In Chart 25, Mars as Lagna lord was not particularly supportive except to delay the event of loss of spouse.

Chart 30 : Born 24-11-1971 at 22h. 55m. (IST) at 28 N 15, 76 E 36 with a balance of 5 years, 0 months and 5 days of Mars Dasa at birth.

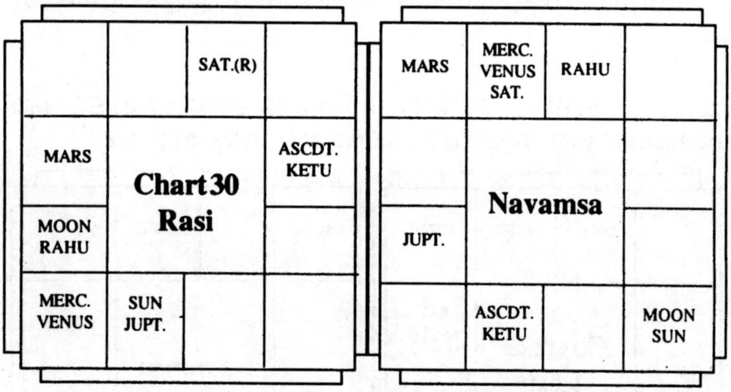

Mars in the 8th in Chart 30 snatched the husband away by death on 27-7-1993 just weeks after the marriage on 5-6-1993. Rahu is in the 7th from the Ascendant too. The affliction from Mars was compounded by Saturn's aspect on him as 8th lord and the fact of Kalatrakaraka Venus coming under a Papakartari Yoga.

There is a school of thought that holds Mars in the 7th is not harmful if aspected by benefics — Jupiter, Venus or Mercury; or if benefics occupy the 4th, 5th, 9th or 10th or even Lagna but themselves should not be in debility, combust or with the Nodes. In other words, Mars in the 7th can be curbed by a benefic in the Ascendant, primarily. This is just an application of Varahamihira's basic principle that Jupiter, Mercury or the Lagna lord in Lagna strengthen the Ascendant and therefore, the horoscope in general.

होरास्वामिगुरुज्ञवीक्षितयुता नान्यैश्च वीर्योत्कटा ।

— **Brihat Jataka,** Chap.1, 19

If the lord of the Lagna, Jupiter or Mercury occupy or aspect the Ascendant, it becomes most powerful. If other than these planets aspect or occupy it, it will not be so.

An Aries Ascendant native with Jupiter in the 1st house and Mars in the 7th did not really suffer from the *Dosha of Mars.* Her husband did die before her but when she was 75 years old.

Likewise, malefics in Lagna can be deemed to aggravate the Dosha of Mars.

In Charts 26, 29 and 30 this holds good. Both Charts 26 and 29 have Saturn in the Ascendant as a strong malefic while Chart 30 has the Nodal axis afflicting the Ascendant and its lord.

Chart 31 : Born 30-6-1972 at 6-10 a.m.

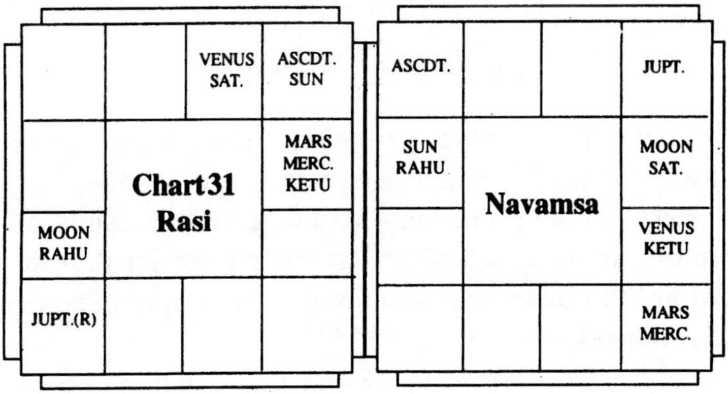

Chart 31 has a strong Kuja Dosha caused not only by malefic Mars in the 2nd from Lagna but also being in the 7th from the Moon. The Sun occupies Lagna. Marriage took place on 14-9-1992 and the girl left the husband on 1-6-1996. She refused to go back to him inspite of his repeated efforts. An *ex-parte* divorce on 6-11-1997 ended the marriage.

Married on 21-6-1983, the native of Chart 32 lost her husband on 25-11-1991 in a jeep accident. Mars occupies the 4th from Lagna while being in the 8th from the Moon. Rahu with Mars aggravates the affliction.

Chart 32: Born 30-6-1961 at 3-47 a.m.

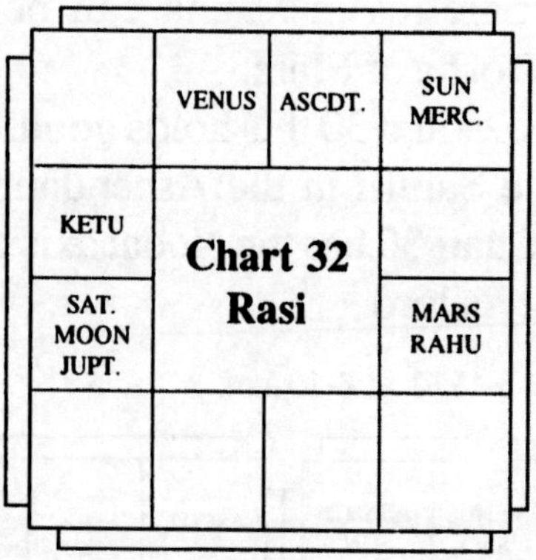

Mars is not the sole agent in curtailing the duration of marital life. Rahu can be equally destructive.

Rahu, although usually said to give the results of Saturn, strangely acts like Mars when placed in the 4th, 7th or 8th houses and to a lesser extent in the 2nd or 12th houses.

In the 7th, like Mars, Rahu can cause death or break up the marriage. In the 8th, however, he becomes fatal to the spouse.

The marriage of the native of Chart 33 took place on 31-5-1989. She was widowed on 26-12-1991. Rahu is in the 8th from Lagna. Saturn in the 7th strengthens this affliction; so does Mars in the 2nd from the Moon and Rahu himself in the 12th from the Moon.

Chart 33 : Born 14-7-1966 at 11-01 a.m. (IST) at 22 N 18, 70 E 56 with a balance of 11 months and 16 days of Sun Dasa at birth.

SAT.	RAHU	MOON VENUS	MARS JUPT. SUN
	Chart 33 Rasi		MERC.
		KETU	ASCDT.

MOON	JUPT.		SUN KETU
	Navamsa		
ASCDT. MARS			
MERC. RAHU			VENUS SAT.

In Chart 32, Rahu in the 8th from the Moon aggravates the evil of Mars in the 8th and, in turn, also gains strength to wreck havoc on the married life of the native.

Rahu in the 7th is not as malefic as in the 8th. But if supported by other Vaidhavya or *para*-Vaidhavya Yogas can become fatal to the spouse.

Another combination that can deal a death blow to the spouse centres round Venus. If malefics flank Venus on either side as in a Papakartari Yoga or occupy the 4th, 8th and 12th from Venus jointly or severally, loss of spouse can occur by death.

Likewise, the 7th lord in the 8th or the 8th lord in the 7th or a Parivartana or exchange of signs between the 7th and 8th lords can snatch away one's spouse. For a Scorpio native, the 7th lord Venus in the 8th brought about widowhood in her forties.

Moving on to the Navamsa, Yogas for widowhood gain strength if a Martian Navamsa is rising.

In Chart 30, widowhood struck within 7 weeks of marriage. Mars occupies the 8th from Lagna. Rahu is in the 7th from the Lagna. Venus is caught between combust Jupiter and eclipsed Moon. The Navamsa rising is Scorpio.

Summing up,

a. Mars in the 1st, 2nd, 4th or 12th damages marital hapiness.

b. Mars in the 7th usually leads to separation and estrangement, rather than death. In exceptional cases, death can occur.

c. Mars in the 8th invariably leads to physical death of spouse.

d. Rahu in the 7th can either lead to death or divorce of spouse.

e. Rahu in the 8th causes death of spouse; in rare cases it can be divorce also.

f. Venus caught in a Papakartari Yoga or with malefics in the 4th, 7th or 8th from him deprives one of marital happiness, usually through death.

These afflictions can be checked by benefics influencing the zone of affliction or by matching with a chart with similar afflictions. ●

Chapter X

Practical Examples of Matching

Example I

Matching of Dosha-free Charts

Chart A: Girl: Born 15-3-1966 at 11-10. a.m. (IST) at 10 N 49, 79 E 50 with a balance of 15 years, 10 months and 15 days of Venus Dasa at birth.

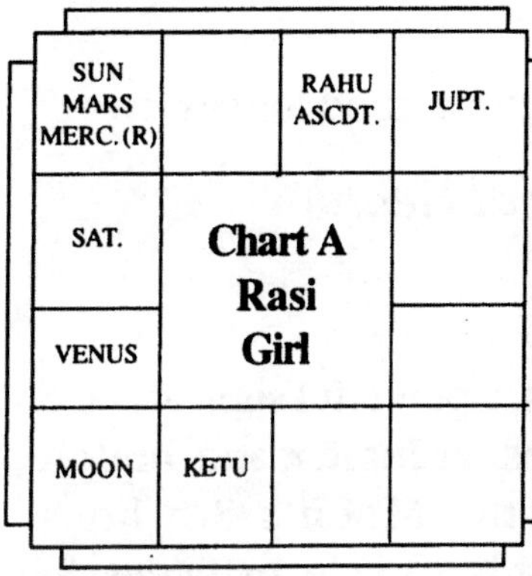

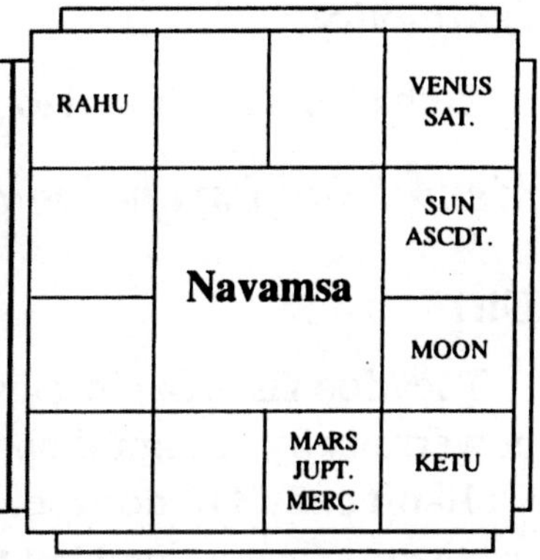

Chart B: Boy: Born 2-6-1963 at 6-59 a.m. at 13 N 05, 80 E 18 with a balance of 1 year, 11 months and 23 days of Moon Dasa at birth.

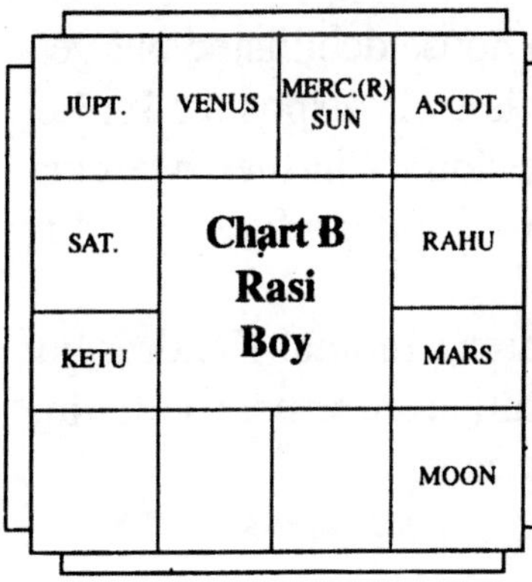

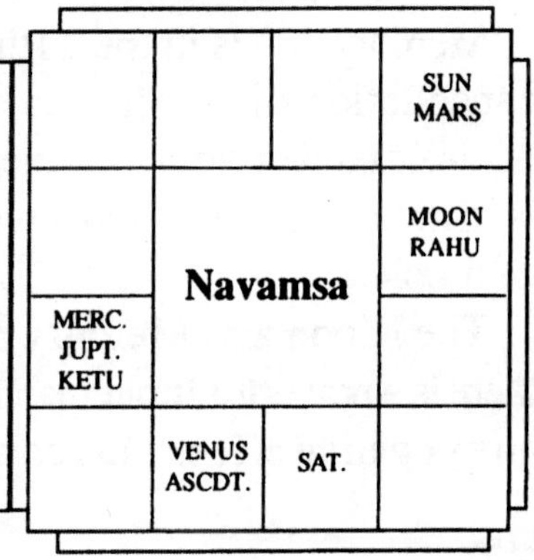

These two charts are a good illustration of matching between Dosha-free charts. The expression

'Dosha-free' does not mean there are absolutely no afflictions in the two charts. It only means there are no heavy afflictions that need to be taken care of.

We shall assess the two charts on the different factors involved.

Longevity

Both charts are found to show good longevity.

Mental and Psychological Health

Girl

The Moon is in Sagittarius, a powerful sign, aspected powerfully by its sign-dispositer Jupiter, and threfore, well-placed. Of course, the Moon's 8th house occupation is not good but this is made up by the sign involved being a highly positive sign Sagittarius as also Jupiter's aspect.

Mercury (R) is in the 11th house debilitated but gets cancellation of debility as his sign-dispositer Jupiter occupies a Kendra from the Moon. Further, Mercury is in an exchange of signs with Jupiter which is highly desirable.

The Moon and Mercury are in mutual Kendras but there is a powerful Jupiterean influence on both nullifying any negative effects this can cause.

Boy

The Moon here too has a powerful Jupiterean influence. Further, the Moon is in the 4th with Digbaḷa.

Mercury, on the other hand, though in the 12th is in a

friendly sign Taurus, free of afflictions.

Both charts, therefore, show sound psychological health.

More Than One Marriage

Girl

Kalatrakaraka Venus is quite well-placed in the 9th in a friendly sign Capricorn. Venus, as Lagna lord, in the 9th favors his signification, that is, marital life.

The 7th lord Mars, though in the 11th, is with benefic Mercury and the Sun and influenced by the 11th lord Jupiter by a Parivartana with Mercury. From the Moon-sign, Jupiter in the 7th is a stabilizing influence both on the 7th house Gemini and 7th lord Mercury.

Boy

The 7th lord Jupiter is in the 10th in his own sign aspected by the Moon and 11th lord Mars. There is no influence of malefics on Venus who is in the 11th. The 11th house connection is balanced by the powerful and congenial influence of Jupiter on the Manahkaraka Moon.

There are factors which cannot harm marital stability.

Dosha Assessment

Girl

From the Ascendant

1. Rahu is in the 1st
2. Ketu is in the 7th

From the Moon

1. Mars is in the 4th
2. The Sun is in the 4th

From Venus

1. Saturn is in the 2nd

Boy

From the Ascendant

1. Rahu is in the 2nd
2. Ketu is in the 8th

From the Moon

1. Mars is in the 12th

From Venus

1. The Sun is in the 2nd
2. Rahu is in the 4th

Both charts are relatively Dosha-free. The Rahu-Ketu axis across the 1st and 7th in the girls' chart is balanced by the Nodal axis across the 2nd and the 8th in the boy's case. Mars (R) in the girl's 4th from the Moon is balanced by Mars in the 12th from the boy's Moon. Mars (R) in the 4th in the girl's chart is diffused of most of his maleficence by the Parivartana involving Jupiter-Mercury. Rahu in the boy's 4th from Venus is offset by Saturn in the 2nd from the girl's Venus.

Kuta Agreement

Girl - Purvashada (1) in Sagittarius Rasi
Boy - Hasta (4) in Virgo Rasi

Varna

Girl - Sagittarius — Kshatriya
Boy - Virgo — Vaishya
Varna Kuta is absent.

Vashya

The girl's Rasi Sagittarius and the boy's Virgo Rasi do not come under the approved pair.

Vashya Kuta is not present.

Dina

Counting from the girl's Nakshatra Poorvashada to the boy's Hasta, we get 21. Dividing 21/9, we get 2 *plus* remainder 3.

Dina Kuta is absent.

Yoni

The girl's comes under male monkey (Purvashada) while the boy's (Hasta) is female buffalo.

Since the Yonis are not inimical, *Yoni Kuta* may be said to be present.

Grahamaitra

The girl's Rasi lord Jupiter and the boy's Rasi lord Mercury are neutrals.

Grahamaitra is present.

Gana

The girl's Nakshatra Purvashada comes under Manushya Gana and the boy's Hasta under Daiva.

Gana Kuta is present.

Rasi

The girl's Janma Rasi Sagittarius is the 4th from the boy's Janma Rasi Virgo.

Rasi Kuta is present.

Nadi

The girl's Nakshatra Purvashada comes under Pittha and the boy's, Hasta, comes under Vata.

Nadi Kuta is present.

Rajju

Poorvashada (girl) comes under Ooru (thigh) and Hasta, under Kanta (neck).

Rajju Kuta is present.

Stree Deergha

The boy's constellation Hasta being the 21st from the girl's Poorvashada, it is beyond the 9th from the latter's.

Stree Deergha is present.

Mahendra

The boy's Nakshatra is the 21st from the girl's Nakshatra.

Mahendra Kuta is absent.

Therefore, *Yoni, Graha, Maitri, Guna, Rasi, Nadi, Rajju* and *Stree Deergha Kutas* are present. Only *Varna, Vashya, Dina* and *Mahendra* are lacking. Therefore, Kuta agreement is present.

Summing up, since :

1. Longevity in both charts is good,
2. Mental and psychological health is sound,
3. Neither chart shows instability in marriage,
4. Kuta agreement is good,

the charts may be said to make a good pair and compatible.

Example II

Matching of Dosha-ridden Charts

Chart C: Boy: Born 30-9-1967 at 8-40 p.m. (IST) at 10 N 49, 79 E 50 with a balance of 6 years, 7 months and 29 days of Ketu Dasa at birth.

SAT. (R)	RAHU LAGNA		
	Chart C Rasi Boy		
			MOON JUPT. VENUS
	MARS	MERC. KETU	SUN

	MOON	SUN JUPT.	VENUS RAHU
	Navamsa		
LAGNA MARS			
MERC JUPT. KETU			

Chart D: Girl: Born 15-7-1971 at 6-30 a.m. at 13 N 05, 80 E 18 with a balance of 3 years, 6 months and 3 days of Mercury Dasa at birth.

MOON		SAT.	VENUS SUN
	Chart D Rasi Girl		MERC. KETU LAGNA
MARS (R) RAHU			
	JUPT.(R)		

MOON VENUS	SAT.		SUN
KETU	Navamsa		
			JUPT. RAHU
			MARS LAGNA

The two charts here have heavy Dosha content.

Longevity

Both have good longevity.

Mental and Psychological Health

Boy

The Moon is extremely well-placed in the royal sign Leo with benefics Venus and Jupiter. The Moon does not receive any adverse aspects and may be said to be placed congenially.

Mercury is in Libra in the 7th with Ketu which is a mild affliction. The Sun and Mars flank Mercury but these two factors may not indicate any psychological difficulties in the boy as the Moon is very well-placed.

Girl

The Moon is quite well-placed in the 9th house aspected by 9th lord Jupiter (R). The Moon is Vargottama which is a *plus* point, especially that he occupies the best trine in strength.

Mercury in this case too is with Ketu and receives the combined aspects of Jupiter, Mars and Saturn. These aspects are all favorable — Mars being exalted, Saturn's being the 3rd house aspect from the 11th and Jupiter's, being a trinal aspect.

The Moon and Mercury are so placed as to give good mental and psychological health.

More Than One Marriage Factor

Boy

The 7th lord Venus in the 5th is well-placed with Jupiter and the Moon. The 6th lord Mercury in the 7th, therefore, does not become harmful.

Venus is also congenially placed and rules out any serious blows to the marital relationship.

From the Moon-sign, the 1st and 7th lords, the Sun and Saturn (R) are in opposition but the 7th from the Moon-sign is favorably aspected by Jupiter.

Girl

The 7th lord Saturn in the 11th is favorably aspected by Jupiter. Venus in the 12th is with Vargottama Sun but unafflicted as the distance between the two is quite wide. The affliction, if any, to Venus from the Sun may be deemed minor.

Dosha Assessment

Boy

From the Lagna

1. Rahu is in the 1st
2. Ketu is in the 7th
3. Mars is in the 8th
4. Saturn is in the 12th

From the Moon

1. The Sun is in the 2nd
2. Mars is in the 4th
3. Saturn (R) is in the 8th

From Venus

1. The Sun is in the 2nd
2. Mars is in the 4th
3. Saturn (R) is in the 8th

Girl

From the Ascendant

1. Ketu is in the 1st
2. Rahu is in the 7th
3. Mars (R) is in the 7th
4. The Sun is in the 12th

From the Moon

1. The Sun is in the 4th

From Venus

1. Ketu is in the 2nd
2. Rahu is in the 8th
3. Mars (R) is in the 8th
4. Saturn is in the 12th

The main Dosha in the two charts come from Mars and the Nodal axis.

The boy's Mars in the 8th from the Ascendant is matched by Mars (R) in the 8th from the girl's Venus.

Mars in the 4th from the boy's Moon and Venus is balanced by Mars in the 7th from the girl's Ascendant.

The boy's Nodal axis across the Lagna is balanced by the axis in the girl's 1st and 7th houses.

Saturn in the 8th and the Sun in the 2nd from the boy's Moon is offset by the Nodal axis across the 2nd and 8th from the girl's Venus.

There is good Dosha Samya between the two charts.

Kuta Agreement

Boy - Makha (1) — Leo Rasi
Girl - Revati (2) — Meena Rasi

Varna

Boy - Leo — Kshatriya

Girl - Pisces — Brahmin

Varna Kuta is absent.

Vashya

Boy - Leo

Girl - Pisces

Vashya Kuta is absent.

Dina

The boy's Nakshatra Makha is the 11th from the girl's Revati. Dividing 11 by 9, we get 1 *plus* 2 remainder which is good.

Dina Kuta is present

Yoni

Boy - Makha — Male rat

Girl - Revati — Female elephant

Since the Yonis are of non-inimical animals and of different sexes, *Yoni Kuta* is present.

Graha Maitra

The boy's Rasi lord Sun and the girl's Rasi lord Jupiter are friends.

Griha Maitra is present.

Gana

Boy - Makha — Rakshasa, but since Venus and Jupiter are with the Moon, the affliction is nullified.

Girl - Revati — Daiva

Gana Kuta is present

Rasi

The boy's Rasi is in the 6th from the girl's which is not favorable.

Rasi Kuta is absent.

Nadi

The boy's Nakshatra comes under Sleshma Nadi and the girl's Revati also under Sleshma Rasi.

Nadi Kuta is absent.

Rajju

Boy - Makha — Pada (foot)
Girl - Revati — Pada (foot)

Rajju Kuta is absent.

Stree Deergha

The boy's constellation Makha is beyond the 9th from the girl's Revati.

Stree Deergha is present.

Mahendra

Mahendra Kuta is not present.

Summing up, *Varna, Vashya, Rasi, Nadi, Rajju and Mahendra Kutas* are absent while *Dina, Yoni, Graha Maitra, Gana* and *Stree Deergha Kutas* are present. Kuta agreement obtains.

In conclusion :

(1) Longevity is good,

(2) Mental and psychological health factors are favorably placed,

(3) Marital stability is good in both charts,

(4) Dosha Samya is present,

(5) Kuta Agreement is passable.

Therefore, both charts, although with strong afflictions or Doshas, are evenly placed and the matching between them may be said to be good.

Example III

A Case of Bad Matching

Chart E : Girl: Born 15-7-1969 at 00-30 a.m. (IST) at 13 N 00, 77 E 35 with a balance of 1 year, 2 months and 15 days of Jupiter Dasa at birth.

RAHU	SAT. LAGNA	VENUS	MERC
MANDI	Chart E Rasi Girl		SUN MOON
	MARS		JUPT. KETU

JUPT.	MERC.	VENUS	LAGNA
	Navamsa		SUN MOON RAHU
KETU			SAT.
	MANDI	MARS	

Chart F: Boy : Born 5-11-1965 at 11-15 p.m. (IST) at 13 N, 77 E 35 with a balance of 9 years, 9 months and 4 days of Saturn Dasa at birth.

MOON		RAHU	JUPT. (R)
SAT. (R)	Chart F Rasi Boy		LAGNA
			MANDI
MARS VENUS	MERC. KETU	SUN	

SAT.	SUN MARS	RAHU	VENUS MANDI
	Navamsa		
JUPT.	KETU	MERC.	MOON LAGNA

These two natives got married with the marriage being celebrated on a grand scale. But the marriage floundered and ended on the rocks. Let us try to see where the problem began astrologically. Of course, the marriage, when it was finalised, did not seek astrological guidance.

Longevity

The longevity in both charts is reasonably good.

Mental and Psychological Health

Girl

The Moon is in a highly emotional sign. The proximity of the Moon at 92^0 19' to the Sun at 90^0 19' in the same sign calls for great care while matching as it makes the native deeply emotional and sensitive. However, the Moon being Vargottama and in his own sign, are *plus* points and indicate a sound state of mind.

Mercury is in the 3rd house aspected by debilitated Saturn and Lagna lord Mars. However, being in his own sign, Gemini is of some help.

Boy

The Moon, who is also the Lagna lord in the 9th house, is in Cancer. This by itself is not bad. But the Moon is aspected by Mars from the 6th house, a Dustana, with Mars being in Moola. Moola is ruled by Ketu and Ketu is in Scorpio with Buddhikaraka Mercury aspected by the unfeeling retrograde Saturn. This gives a tendency to inflict pain and suffering on others and is not a desirable planetary feature.

Mercury is in the 5th with Ketu and aspected

powerfully by malefic retrograde Saturn which is again not a happy feature.

More than One Marriage Factor

Moving on to the question of, if either chart carries clues to *more than one marriage* and therefore, *jeopardy to the first* marriage, we find the girl's Venus is Vargottama and quite well-placed in the 2nd house in his own sign. But Saturn as 10th and, more significantly, as 11th lord is in the Ascendant aspecting the 7th house which makes the chart vulnerable to instability in marriage. Further, there is Mars in the 8th from the Ascendant and in the 7th from Kalatrakaraka Venus which are factors that require to be balanced in the groom's chart. Minor afflictions are the Sun in the 4th and Rahu in the 12th from the Ascendant.

Moving on to the boy's chart, the 7th lord Saturn is in the 8th retrograde. Even if in his own sign and Moolatrikona Aquarius, the retrogression of the 7th lord is a factor that calls for caution. The Kalatrakaraka Venus is in the 6th with Mars aspected by Jupiter (R) from the 12th, also from a common sign. The Ascendant lord Moon too is in Pisces, another dual sign. These are all factors which distinctly point to more than one marriage implying the first marriage may not last.

Dosha Assessment

Girl

From the Ascendant

1. Saturn (debilitated) is in the 1st
2. The Sun occupies the 4th

3. Mars is in the 8th from the Ascendant
4. Rahu is in the 12th

From the Moon

1. The Sun is in the 1st

From Venus

1. Mars is in the 7th
2. Saturn is in the 12th

Boy

From the Ascendant

1. The Sun (in debility) is in the 4th
2. Saturn (R) is in the 8th

From the Moon

1. The Sun (in debility) is in the 4th
2. Saturn (R) is in the 8th

From Venus

1. Mars (R) is in the 1st
2. Ketu is in the 12th

Afflictions in the boy's chart center round the Sun in the 4th and Saturn in the 8th which may be described as too mild to keep at bay Mars in the 8th from Lagna and in the 7th from Venus in the girl's chart.

Further, Saturn in the Ascendant, especially in this case, as the Lagna happens to be Aries, is a major drawback in the girl's chart.

Kuta Agreement

Girl - Punarvasu (4) in Cancer Rasi
Boy - Uttarabhadrapada (2) in Pisces Rasi

Varna

Girl - Cancer — Brahmin
Boy - Pisces — Brahmin
Varna Kuta is present.

Vashya

Vashya Kuta is not present

Dina

Counting the girl's Nakshatra Punarvasu from the boy's Uttarabhadrapada, we get 16. Dividing 16 by 9, we get remainder 7.

Therefore, *Dina Kuta* is not present

Yoni

Girl - Punarvasu (female cat)
Boy - Uttarabhadrapada (female cow)
The Yonis are not of different sexes and therefore, *Yoni Kuta* is not satisfactory.

Graha Maitra

The girl's Moon-sign lord is the Moon and the boy's Jupiter. The Moon is neutral to Jupiter and Jupiter is friendly to the Moon.

Graha Maitra is present.

Gana

Girl - Punarvasu—Daiva
Boy - Uttarabhadrapada — Manushya

Gana Kuta is passable.

Rasi

The Janma Rasi of the girl is the 5th from the boy's which is good.

Rasi Kuta is present.

Nadi

Girl - Punarvasu — Vata
Boy - Uttarabhadrapada — Pittha
Nadi Kuta is present.

Rajju

Girl - Punarvasu — Nabhi (navel)
Boy - Uttarabhadrapada — Ooru (thigh)
Rajju Kuta is present.

Stree Deergha

The boy's constellation being the 20th, *Stree Deergha* is present.

Mahendra

Girl - Punarvasu
Boy - Uttarabhadrapada
The boy's constellation being the 20th from the girl's, *Mahendra Kuta* is absent.

Therefore, in this case, Kuta agreement occurs in *Varna, Graha Maitra, Gana, Rasi, Nadi, Rajju and Stree Deergha* — in 6 factors in all.

Kuta agreement is lacking in *Vashya, Dina, Yoni* and *Mahendra* — 4 factors.

As a rule, if at least 5 factors obtain, then Kuta

agreement may be deemed to be present.

Therefore, *Kuta agreement* is present.

Summing up,

1) Longevity is good,
2) The boy's psychological health is not satisfactory,
3) Dosha Samya is lacking,
4) The girl's chart shows instability while the boy'a chart indicates more than one marriage.

The more important factors of psychological health, Dosha Samya and more than one marriage being unsatisfactory, the horoscopic compatibility between the two natives is badly lacking.

The couple left for the United States soon after the marriage. But the girl was in for a shock, as day by day she found her husband's ill-treatment growing worse. Traumatised and unable to bear it any longer, she fled to a family friend's place, and from there, returned to India to her parents. She was able to obtain divorce shortly after.

Pairing with a Suitable Chart

This same girl got married a second time on 26-7-1998 to a gentle and amicable highly qualified divorcee.

In this case, the groom who had been married earlier on 2-12-1993 had obtained a divorce on 18-6-1998. He married the native of Chart E at a simple ceremony and now, both are happily settled in the U.S.A.

Chart G: Husband: Born 19-6-1969 at 11-18 a.m. (IST) at 17 N 22, 78 E 26 with a balance of 9 years, 7 months and 3 days of Mercury Dasa at birth.

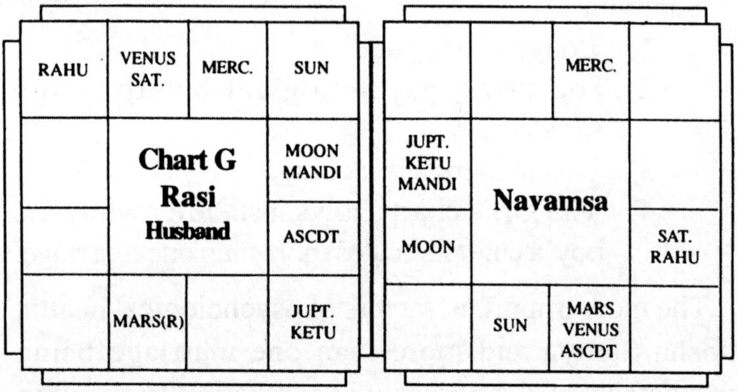

Longevity

Longevity in both charts is good.

Mental and Psychological Health

The boy has Moon in Cancer in his own sign free of aspects and association. There are no afflictions to the Moon by aspect or association which testifies to the congenial state of mind of the boy. Mercury is in the 10th Vargottama in a friendly sign and aspected by Mars (R) and Jupiter. Mercury is not afflicted in any way.

More Than One Marriage Factor

The 7th lord Saturn is in the 9th in debility and with Karaka Venus. The affliction to Venus can result in the first marriage breaking up.

Dosha Assessment

From the Ascendant

1. Ketu is in the 2nd house
2. Mars (R) is in the 4th house
3. Rahu is in the 8th house

From the Moon

1. The Sun is in the 12th house

From Venus

1. Saturn (in debility) is in the 1st house
2. Mars is in the 8th house
3. Rahu is in the 12th house

Comparing these Dosha factors with those in the girl's chart, that due to Mars (R) in the 8th from Venus and of Saturn in the 1st from Venus in the boy's, balance the same two afflictions in the girl's chart from the Ascendant. The girl additionally has Mars in the 7th from Venus which is balanced by retrograde Mars in the 4th from Lagna in the boy's chart.

Further, in both charts, the first marriages have failed and this fact must be borne in mind in evaluating the balancing of Dosha in these charts.

Kuta Agrement

Girl - Punarvasu (4) in Cancer Rasi

Boy - Aslesha (3) in Cancer Rasi

The boy and girl both have common Janma Rasi but the Nakshatra of the girl precedes that of the boy which is not forbidden. But let us also look at the other Kuta details.

Varna

Both come under Cancer showing Brahmin which is desirable.

Varna Kuta is present.

Vashya

Vashya Kuta is absent.

Dina

The boy's Nakshatra is the 3rd from the girl's.

Dina Kuta is absent.

Yoni

Girl - Punarvasu — female cat

Boy - Aslesha — male cat

Since both belong to the same animal and different sexes, *Yoni Kuta* is present.

Graha Maitra

Both the boy and the girl have the same Janma Rasi, and therefore, the same planet Moon as their Rasi lord.

Grahamaitra is present.

Gana

Girl - Punarvasu (Daiva)

Boy - Aslesha (Rakshasa)

However, the Moon being free of adverse influences, the Rakshasa Gana can be reined in.

Gana Kuta is absent.

Rasi

The Janma Rasis are in the same sign.

Rasi Kuta is present.

Nadi

Girl - Punarvasu (vata)
Boy - Aslesha (Sleshma)
Nadi Kuta is present.

Rajju

Girl - Punarvasu — Nabhi (navel)
Boy - Aslesha — Pada (foot)
Rajju Kuta is present.

Stree Deergha

Since the boy's constellation is the 3rd from the girl's, *Stree Deergha* is absent.

Mahendra

For the same reason, *Mahendra Kuta* too is absent.

In this pair, Kuta agreement is present in *Varna, Yoni, Grahamaitra, Rasi, Nadi* and *Rajju* while it is lacking in *Vashya, Dina, Gana, Stree Deergha* and *Mahendra.*

Kuta agreement occurs in 6 factors which is a good score.

The more important factors of psychological health, Dosha Samya and the more than one marriage factor being compatible, the match between this pair can be said to be good.

Example IV

Dangerous Charts

Chart H: Girl: Born 9-9-1968 at 3-40 a.m. (IST) at 22 N 35, 88 E 21 with balance of 14 years, 10 months and 7 days of Mercury Dasa at birth.

MOON 18-21 RAHU 18-41	SAT.		
	Chart H Rasi Girl		LAGNA MARS
			JUPT. SUN
			MERC. VENUS KETU

MARS	LAGNA SAT.	VENUS	MERC.
	Navamsa		
MOON	JUPT.	SUN	

Chart I : Boy: Born 28-9-1964 at 23h. at 31 N 49, 76 E 32 with a balance of 6 years, 8 months and 22 days of Rahu Dasa at birth.

		JUPT. 3-54	LAGNA MOON 15-01 RAHU 05-01
SAT. (R)	**Chart I Rasi Boy**		MARS
			VENUS 0-10
KETU			SUN 13-42 MERC 0-33

	VENUS	SUN KETU	
MOON JUPT.	**Navamsa**		
LAGNA MERC.			
SAT.	MARS RAHU		

Longevity and Mental Health

Girl

The Ascendant Cancer has its ruler Moon in the 9th,

a trine aspected by natural benefics Mercury and Venus. But a closer look will reveal the Moon is in exact degree conjunction with Rahu. Such a planetary disposition should at once make one sit up and check for negative factors.

Natural malefics, Mars and Saturn, are in the 1st and 10th Kendras, both in their signs of debilitation. No benefics occupy the Kendras. Jupiter is combust.

Such a planetary set-up can indicate some serious deficiency in the mind or the body. Her, the Moon, though with Rahu is aspected by Mercury and Venus, both natural benefics. But again, Mercury in mutual aspect with the Moon, is never desirable in the absence of strong balancing features.

The Ascendant is heavily afflicted by malefics in Kendras with no redeeming influences with the Moon as the Ascendant lord also afflicted. Therefore, this brings the physical body and well-being of the girl in question. In other words, longevity becomes highly doubtful.

Boy

The Ascendant Gemini is afflicted by the Moon and the presence of Rahu in it. The Ascendant lord Mercury in the 4th in his sign of exaltation is in a cuspal degree. No benefics occupy the Kendras with only the Nodes and the Sun in Kendras. This chart too, therefore, becomes deficient in terms of both mental and physical well-being. The mutual Kendra positions of the afflicted Moon and Mercury must be taken note of as well as the Ascendant sign occupied by the Moon and Rahu.

Jupiter's aspect on Mercury is from the 12th house and a slight relief.

Therefore, not only do both charts show poor longevity but also highly complex psychological personalities. Of course, the girl's is better than boy's as far as mental health goes.

Therefore, such charts must be marked out as incapable of normal life, especially marital life.

Let us, however, go through the entire process of matching and see where the whole thing stands.

More Than One Marriage

Girl

Five planets out of 9 factors are in common signs *plus* a badly afflicted Moon. Venus, Mercury and Ketu are in the 7th from the Moon in a common sign which rules out stability or durability of marital life.

Boy

The Ascendant Gemini has the 2nd lord Moon in it with Rahu. The Ascendant lord Mercury is in the 4th in a common sign with the Sun but with some relief from Jupiter's aspect. But Jupiter as 7th lord in the 12th is not a happy feature, especially that the Lagna and the Moon are both afflicted by the Nodes. Marital life does not appear to be sound or stable in this case.

Dosha Assessment

Girl

From the Lagna

1. Mars (in debility) is in the 1st
2. The Sun is in the 2nd

From the Moon

1. Rahu is in the 1st
2. Saturn is in the 2nd
3. Ketu is in the 7th

From Venus

1. Ketu is in the 1st
2. Rahu is in the 7th
3. Saturn is in the 8th
4. The Sun is in the 12th

Boy

From the Lagna

1. Rahu is in the 1st
2. Mars (in debility) is in the 2nd
3. The Sun is in the 4th
4. Ketu is in the 7th

From the Moon

Same as for the Lagna

From Venus

1. The Sun is in the 2nd
2. Saturn (R) is in the 7th
3. Mars (in debility) is in the 12th

The afflictions are about the same and evenly distributed.

The Nodal axis afflicts the Moon-sign of the girl and the Ascendant *plus* Moon-sign of the boy, the latter being more weighty. But this is offset by the Nodal affliction to Venus in the girl's case.

Mars in the 1st of the girl's is balanced by Mars in the 2nd from the boy's, but since it occurs also with reference to the Moon-sign, the boy's Dosha exceeds the girl's.

Saturn in the 8th from the girl's Venus is balanced by Saturn in the 7th from the boy's.

Kuta Agreement

Girl - Revati (1) -Pisces

Boy - Aridra (3) - Gemini

Varna

Girl - Pisces — Brahmin

Boy - Gemini — Sudra

Varna Kuta is absent.

Vashya

Gemini and Pisces have no Vashya.

Vashya Kuta is absent.

Dina

Girl - Revati

Boy - Aridra

Counting from the girl's Nakshatra (Revati) to the boy's constellation Aridra, we get 7 which is not good.

Dina Kuta is absent.

Yoni Kuta

Girl - Revati — Female elephant

Boy - Aridra — female dog

Yoni Kuta is absent.

Grahamaitra

Girl - Pisces — Jupiter

Boy - Gemini — Mercury

Mercury and Jupiter are neutrals.

Grahamaitra is present.

Gana

Girl - Revati — Daiva
Boy - Aridra — Manushya
Gana Kuta is present.

Raśi

The boy's Janma Rasi Gemini is in the 4th from the girl's Janma Rasi Pisces and is not desirable.

Rasi Kuta is absent.

Nadi

Girl - Revati — Sleshma
Boy - Aridra — Vata
Nadi Kuta is present.

Rajju

Girl - Revati—Pada (feet)
Boy - Aridra — Kanta (neck)
Rajju Kuta is present.

Stree Deergha

The Boy's Nakshatra Aridra is the 7th from Revati, the girl's Nakshatra.

Stree Deergha is absent.

Mahendra

Revati to Aridra = 7
Mahendra Kuta is present.

Graha Maitra, Gana, Rasi, Nadi, Rajju and *Mahendra Kutas* are present which is quite a good score.

But this assessement takes no note of the basic structure of the charts, either in terms of longevity or mental health, the primary and most important considerations while matching and therefore, if taken as conclusive, can be misleading.

This example is a good illustration of how improper assessment of charts based only on Kuta agreement can lead to tragic consequence as will be evident from the following facts of the case :

The girl got married on 6-3-1992 to the man she had fallen in love with, despite stiff opposition from her family. Following ill-treatment from her in-laws, she took an overdose of sleeping tablets on 30-5-1993. She survived but went back to her parents on 11-6-1993. When even after a year and a half, no one from her husband's family contacted her, her family filed a dowry case against them. Two brothers-in-law were taken into custody for 28 days as a result. Some mediation by her in-laws followed after which she went back to them on 10-9-1994. She took up a teaching job. She was allegedly murdered by her husband in her flat at Bhubaneswar on 18-10-1997 at about 4-30 p.m. by her throat being slit. The husband was taken into police custody on 20-10-1997. ●

Chapter XI

Some Questions Answered

XI

Question: *Many eligible alliances are rejected simply becuase the horoscopes are not found satisfactory. Is it not unfair to the parties concerned and does it not amount to spoiling the marital prospects of the young boy and girl who may be eager to get married ?*

Answer: This is a very interesting question and whole tomes can be written before coming up with a complete answer. However, to be brief, there are two angles to this question.

If by 'eligible' is meant social status, family background and such other factors, then marriages made only on these assessments should have been highly successful which is far from true. Your question is akin to asking a doctor to overlook the diagnosis of a terminal ailment in the patient so that his mental peace and / or marital prospects are not disturbed. Would a doctor, when he finds a young man or woman testing HIV positive, refrain from divulging it because it would mar their prospects of marriage ? But, in astrology, unlike in medical diagnosis, when an affliction is pointed out, it is done with a view to help the natives involved avoid a disastrous marriage. Because a chart has a certain affliction, it does not mean it is an absolute write-off of the marriage. Rather, it is a warning to be careful with the instruction that if paired with a suitable chart, a normal marital life can be ensured.

Question: *Many a time, it is found that the compatibility of the boy and girl works out to an excellent score of 25 points or above out of 36 points. Yet, these marriages break off or disintegrate in a couple of years and sometimes, within months. For example, in the case of a tragic marriage, the compatibility between the girl — Uttarabhadrapada (4) and the boy, Poorvabhadrapada (4) — came to 33 out of 36 points. Why did the marriage end in divorce inspite of such good matching ?*

Answer: If you have gone through the entire text of this book, you will find that the matching rules have not been applied at all. Matching is a long drawn process and takes into accounts several important factors. The test of Kuta agreement on which the match in question was made is not the *all of matching.* It is only one of several factors involved in the matching process and is not a decisive one. At best, it can be described as about only 10 percent of the total process of matching. Naturally, results have gone awry.

Question: *It is said that girls born under Moola (1) Aslesha (1), Jyeshta (1) and Visakha (4) are likely to be adverse to the father-in-law, mother-in-law, husband's eldest brother and the husband's youngest brother respectively. In fact, this is given so much importance that girls born in these Nakshatras are rejected outright. In some cases, the families of the girls themselves try to locate proposals where the respective relative is either dead or not* *available. For example, the parents of an Aslesha girl try to find a groom whose mother may be dead. Likewise, in the case of a Moola born girl, they may try alliances where the boy has no father. In the case of a Jyeshta or Visakha girl, they may concentrate on locating a groom who may have no elder or younger brother respectively. How far is this belief justified and what is the solution for such Nakshatras ?*

Answer: Almost all classical works that touch on matching for marriage talk of these 4 Nakshatras and their connection with the respective relatives of the groom. But these are very broad generalisations and cannot be applied literally.

However, the connection cannot be disputed either. But, one must note the connection is not a cause and effect connection. If a statistical study is made, then one would not be surprised to note that the respective relatives have, indeed, been adversely affected after the marriage, more in the case of girls coming under the specified Nakshtras than in the case of those born in Nakshtras other than these. The adversity, however, would also be indicated independently in the relative's chart too.

Secondly, if the girl's chart is otherwise strong and well-placed, the adversity may not show up. In such cases, the respective relative's chart will also be quite safe.

Coming to the second part of your question, the approach itself is highly defective. What a parent should concentrate on is the compatibility of horoscopic factors between the girl and the boy and not extraneous factors, such as the absence or death of relatives of the boy. Because, when one takes such factors as the criterion for the match, one is making the major mistake of assuming all other astrological factors — longevity, mental health, balancing of Dosha — are sound which in fact may not be the case. If the astrological factors are assessed carefully and completely, then there is no need to pay undue attention to the Nakshatra of the girl coming under one of these four Nakshatras.

Question: *What is Dasa Sandhi ? How important is it in matching?*

Answer: Dasa Sandhi is given great importance in certain parts of South India. The Dasas in the charts of the boy and the girl are drawn up. About 5 Dasas after the Dasa at birth would normally suffice. The Dasa-ending periods in the two charts are then checked to ensure they do not end within the span of one year. For example, in the case of a couple, the man's Venus Dasa is due to end in November 2001. The wife's Jupiter Dasa is due to end in January 2001. That means, the respective Dasas in their lives end within a gap of 12 months. Unexpected problems have hit the couple. The husband's career crashed overnight leaving him shattered and humiliated. The stress the couple is undergoing is tremendous because of Dasa Sandhi. Therefore, in order to avoid major calamities, the Dasa Sandhi is also checked. However, if the main factors in matching charts have been found to be good, then even if there is Dasa Sandhi, the difficulties associated with it can be overcome.

Question: *It is said there should be no three Jyeshtas in a marriage. What does this mean ?*

Answer: Tri-Jyeshta Dosha is the concurring of three Jyeshtas at a marriage and is to be avoided at all costs. The lunar month of Jyeshta usually occurs between May and June each year. Jyeshta Masa is, in fact, considered desirable for a marriage Muhurtha. But in such a case, if the birth Nakshatra is Jyeshta or if either the boy or the girl is the eldest (Jyeshta) child in the respective family, then there can be said to be concurrence of three Jyeshtas — the lunar month, the Janma Nakshtra and the boy (or girl) being the *jyeshta* (eldest in the respective family). Such a concurrence is to be avoided if the marriage and the families involved should be happy. Marriage in Jyeshta Nakshatra for a Muhurtha also, as a rule, is forbidden.

Question: *Sometimes, birth charts may not be available. This can happen in cases where the birth time may not have been recorded at all. How can compatibility between the couple be tested ?*

Answer: According to several classical works such as **Vidya Madhaveeyam, Prasna Sangraha** and **Prasna Marga**, the compatibility of a pair can be examined on the basis of the Prasna chart. Of course, in such cases, the framing of the question should be appropriate. A question, "Will this proposal be conducive to a happy and long marriage ?" would be quite properly putting the whole thing. Or, one may even ask "Can A (girl) marry B (boy) ?"

The chart for the time of question is cast and the interpretation may be made based on general principles of hoary astrology or Prasna.

Benefics aspecting the Ascendant, especially from the 7th house, indicate the proposed match can be happy.

Malefics in the 7th aspecting the Ascendant are a warning against the match indicating unhappiness or termination of the marriage.

Jupiter, Venus, Mercury associated with benefics or the Ascendant lord in the 7th are conducive to the match.

Likewise, the Sun, Mars, Saturn or heavily afflicted Mercury in the 7th are not indicative of happiness in the proposed match.

The Moon in the 6th or the 8th from the Prasna Ascendant cautions against the match. If at the same time, Mars occupies the 6th or 8th from the Moon, it shows death of one of the proposed pair. If the Moon and Mars occupy the 7th, then also it shows dire calamity to one of the parties.

If the Kalatrakaraka Venus is well-placed in an Upachaya (the 3rd, 6th, 10th or 11th houses) and so also the 7th lord, it endorses the match in question.

If the Ascendant, the 5th, the 8th and the 9th houses are associated with or aspected by their respective lords, and are devoid of malefic aspects and associations, then also the match can be recommended.

If the Ascendant and the Moon are in benefic signs in the Navamsa, then also it is favorable for the match.

Question: *What is Nama Nakshatra Kuta ? How far can it be relied upon for matching ?*

Answer: Sometimes, there are absolutely no particulars of birth available including the date of birth. At such times, matching may be considered on the basis of the names of the boy and the girl. Most classical works on astrology that deal with Muhurtha carry a table where each Pada of the 27 Nakshatras is identified with a syllable.

Using this table, one can locate the Nakshatra Pada, and therefore, the Rasi of an individual.

Let us take the case of a proposal where the boy is Kartik and the girl is Mythili.

The first syllable in the boy's name is *Ka* (का) for which the Nakshatra is Mrigasira (3). The first syllable in the girl's name is *My* (मै) which is Makha (4). The compatibility between these two Nakshatras on the basis of the Kuta agreement factors is passable. As a confirmation, a Prasna chart can also be erected and analysed before approving the match.

Table of Nama Nakshatras

1.	चु	चे	चो	ला .... अश्विनि
	ಚು	ಚೆ	ಚೋ	ಲಾ .... ಅಶ್ವಿನಿ
	Chu	Chay	Cho	La .... Aswini

2. लि लु ले लो ....भरणि
ಲಿ ಲು ಲೆ ಲೋ .... ಭರಣಿ
Li Lu Lay Lo.................. Bharani

3. आ इ उ ए .... कृत्तिका
ಆ ಇ ಉ ಎ ....ಕೃತ್ತಿಕಾ
A0 Ee U A.................. Krittika

4. ओ वा वी वो .... रोहिणि
ಓ ವಾ ವೀ ವೊ .... ರೋಹಿಣಿ
O Va Vee Vo................... Rohini

5. वे वो का के .... मृगशिरा
ವೇ ವೋ ಕಾ ಕೇ .... ಮೃಗಶಿರಾ
Vay Vo Kaa Ke....:......... Mrigasira

6. कू घा ङ· छ .... आरिद्रा
ಕೂ ಘಾ ಙ ಛ ....ಆರಿದ್ರಾ
Koo Ghaa Gnja Cha .... Aridra

7. के को हा ही .... पुनर्वसु
ಕೆ ಕೋ ಹಾ ಹೀ .... ಪುನರ್ವಸು
Kay Ko Haa Hee.............Punarvasu

8. हू हे हो डा ....पुष्यमी
ಹೂ ಹೇ ಹೋ ಡಾ .... ಪುಷ್ಯಮೀ
Hoo Hay Ho Daa .... Pushyami

9. डी डू डे डो .... आश्लेषा
ಡೀ ಡೂ ಡೇ ಡೋ ....ಆಶ್ಲೇಷಾ
Dee Doo, Day Do ....Aslesha

10. मा मी मू मे ....मखा
ಮಾ ಮೀ ಮೂ ಮೇ..........................ಮಖಾ
Maa Mee Moo May ....Makha

11. मो टा टी दू ...... पूर्वफल्गुणि
ಮೋ ಟಾ ಟೀ ಟೂ .... ಪೂರ್ವಫಲ್ಗುಣಿ(ಪುಬ್ಬ)
Mo Taa Tee Too .... Pubba

12. टे टो पा पी .... उत्तरा
ಟೇ ಟೋ ಪಾ ಪೀ .... ಉತ್ತರಾ
Tay To Paa Pee .... Uttara

13. पू षा ण ठा .... हस्ता
ಪು ಷಾ ಣಾ ಠಾ .... ಹಸ್ತಾ
Pu Shaa Naa Taa .... Hasta

14. पे पो रा री .... चित्ता
ಪೇ ಪೋ ರಾ ರೀ .... ಚಿತ್ತಾ
Pay Po Raa Ree .... Chitta

15. रु रे रा ता .... स्वाती
ರು ರೇ ರಾ ತಾ .... ಸ್ವಾತಿ
Ru Ray Raa Tha .... Swati

16. ती तू ते तो .... विशाखा
ತೀ ತೂ ತೇ ತೋ .... ವಿಶಾಖಾ
Thee Thoo Thay Tho .... Visakha

17. ना नी नू ने .... अनुराधा
ನಾ ನೀ ನೂ ನೇ .... ಅನುರಾಧಾ
Naa Nee Noo Nay .... Anuradha

18. नो या यी यू ....ज्येष्ठा
ನೋ ಯಾ ಯೀ ಯೂ .... ಜ್ಯೇಷ್ಠಾ
No Yaa Yee Yoo .... Jyeshta

19. ये यो बा बी ....मूला
ಯೇ ಯೋ ಬಾ ಬೀ .... ಮೂಲಾ
Yay Yo Baa Bee ....Moola

20. बु धा भ ढा .... पूर्वाषाढा
ಬು ಧಾ ಭ ಢಾ ....ಪೂರ್ವಾಷಾಢಾ
Bu Dhaa Bha Dha .... Poorvashada

21. बे बो जा जी ....उत्तराषाढा
ಬೇ ಬೋ ಜಾ ಜೀ ....ಉತ್ತರಾಷಾಢಾ
Bay Bo Jaa Jee .... Uttarashada

22. जु जे जो घ .... श्रवण
ಜು ಜೆ ಜೋ ಘ ....ಶ್ರವಣ
Ju Jay Jo Gha .... Sravana

23. गा गी गू गे .... धनिष्ठा
ಗಾ ಗೀ ಗೂ ಗೇ ....ಧನಿಷ್ಠಾ
Gaa Gee Goo Gay ....Dhanishta

24. गो सा सी सू .... शतभिष
ಗೋ ಸಾ ಸೀ ಸೂ .... ಶತಭಿಷ
Go Saa See Soo ....Satabhisha

25. से सो दा दी .... पूर्वाभाद्र
ಸೇ ಸೋ ದಾ ದೀ ....ಪೂರ್ವಾಭಾದ್ರ
Say So Daa Dee .... Poorvabhadra

26. दु थ ज्ञ .... उत्तराभाद्र
ದು ಥ ಜ್ಞ ....ಉತ್ತರಾಭಾದ್ರ
Du Tha Jna .... Uttarabhadra

27.	दे	दो	चा	ची .... रेवति
	ದೇ	ದೋ	ಚಾ	ಚೀ .... ರೇವತಿ
	De	Do	Chaa	Chee .... Revati

Question: *Can a chart that shows loss of spouse be handled effectively by a chart where there is no loss indicated ? For example, why not pair a chart with Mars in the 8th with another chart which has good longevity as also stable married life indicated in it ?*

Likewise, what would be the outcome if the chart of a boy with short life indications is matched with that of a girl with a long married life ?

My uncle's son died in about September-October 1962. A marriage alliance came for him while he was about 17 years and still in college. A local astrologer said that the horoscopes of the boy and the girl matched well in all respects. But, he failed to examine and point out the Alpayus (short life) in the boy's chart.

My uncle's son, though inwardly desirous of marriage with this girl, could not do so because of two reasons. He had to still complete his studies and secondly, his parents too were not willing to go ahead with the proposal for one reason or the other. The girl, then only 14 years old, was said to be eager to marry the boy.

Unfortunately, the boy, while studying in B.T. (equivalent to B.Ed.), died unexpectedly of smallpox in 1962. The astrologer who recommended the alliance said that if the marriage had been performed, the boy would have been alive because of the Mangalya Bala in the girl's chart.

Kindly clarify if this would have been possible. Can the short life of a boy who marries a girl whose chart has strong Mangalaya Bala be saved and extended to long life ? Is there any sanction or authority in the classical works for such a match ?

Chart : Boy: Born 31-12-1940 at 0-25 a.m. (IST) at 8 N 45, 77 E 43 with a balance of 9 years, 0 month and 9 days of Venus Dasa at birth.

KETU 15-11	JUPT. 14-15 SAT. 16-42		
	Rasi Boy		
			MOON 20-38
SUN 7-11	MERC 25-09 VENUS 8-23	MARS 28-21	ASCDT. 9-06 RAHU 15-11

ASCDT.		RAHU	SUN MARS
MERC.	Navamsa		
			JUPT.
	KETU	MOON	VENUS SAT.

Chart : Girl: Born 21-10-1943 at 12-45 p.m. at 8 N 45, 77 E 4 with a balance of 12 years, 5 months and 27 days of Saturn Dasa at birth.

			MARS 0-15 SAT. 4-56
	Rasi Girl		MOON 7-54 RAHU 20-21
LAGNA 8-18 KETU 20-21			JUPT 1-20 VENUS 22-04
		SUN 5-24	MERC. 22-10

LAGNA	JUPT.		
	Navamsa		MERC. KETU
RAHU			MOON
	SAT. SUN	MARS VENUS	

Answer: This is a speculative question and an experiment on these lines may prove both costly and tragic. The antidote for Dosha primarily stems from the mathematical truth that two *minuses* make one *plus*. It is also known that *plus* and *minus* never make *plus* but only *minus* and this applies equally well to astrological matching of charts too.

Such a match has no astrological sanction. Extending the underlying principle on tackling Kuja Dosha to other Doshas also, balancing of Doshas can help to tackle the Doshas by either minimising their impact or intensity or by diffusing them. Linking a Dosha-ridden chart with a no-Dosha chart is not the solution.

In this particular case, the marriage did not materialise. The boy died in his youth. As for the girl, she got married in 1960 to a clerk who retired from service in 1992. Both the girl and her husband are living and have 4 daughters but no son. The lady's married life has been happy and long.

In the chart of the lady, the 8th and 9th houses have benefics in them, which tend to protect her Mangalya Bhava or coverture. However, going back to the question if a match between these two charts could have saved the boy, it cannot be answered in the affirmative. There is no sanction for such a match in classical works.

Three combinations from classical works can be quoted in this context.

1. When a girl has malefics in the 7th and 8th houses, a benefic in the 9th will give a long and happy married life.

2. A benefic in the 8th house, if free from malefic influences by aspect or conjunction, generally does not allow the spouse to pre-decease the native.

3. If both malefic and benefic planets occupy the 8th house, the deaths of the native and the spouse occur about the same time. If all other factors are also supportive, then in some cases, death can occur at the same time or about the same time or within a maximum time gap of twelve months.

Question: *Some say that if one has Rahu in the 7th, it is a major affliction showing a miserable marriage but if such a native goes in for an inter-caste marriage, the affliction gets diffused. Is it the correct way to overcome this affliction ?*

Answer: This question only points to the several misconceptions prevailing in the minds of people. Rahu in the 7th can, if not handled properly, give an unhappy marriage. Most times, this affliction tends to give marriage out of one's caste, community or even race. Alternately, it can indicate marriage with a cousin, mostly maternal. However, simply because such a marriage is contracted, does not mean the affliction is overcome. There are countless cases where such an affliction has caused havoc in the marriage, irrespective of whether it is an unconventional one or with a maternal relative. Rahu in the 7th has to be balanced by a like Dosha in the other chart.

Question: *Which are the Maha Nakshatras and why are they given a special status in matching of charts ?*

Answer: According to **Kala Vidhana,**

स्वाती शशांक् पितृतारक मैत्रभानं
पुंर्क्षमस्ति यदि वा वनितर्क्षमस्ति ।
तेषां दिनादि गणनादशकं नचेत्स्यात्
अत्यन्तमिषृ मिति शास्त्रविदो वदान्ति।।

meaning,

should the birth star of either the bride or the groom happen to be Swati, Mrigasira, Makha or Anuradha, they will match very well even if all the ten Kutas do not agree.

Mrigasira, Makha, Swati and Anuradha are known as Maha Nakshatras. They are extolled as being auspicious, and therefore, capable of overriding Kuta agreement considerations. For example, the Kuta agreement between Chitta (3) in Libra Rasi and Anuradha (in Scorpio) is dismally poor. But as Anuradha is one of the Maha Nakshatras, the results of the Kuta test can be ignored. The Maha Nakshatras have an unusual resilience and can overcome problems associated with a poor count in the Kuta agreement test. But it is important to remember that merely becasue one is born in a Maha Nakshatra, it does not insure one against the other defective factors of inadequate longevity, mental and psychological personality imbalances, vulnerability to more than one partner or absence of a balance in the malefic content of the two charts. Only after all these factors have been found to be okay, can the special status of Maha Nakshatras be recognised.

***Question** : Matching of charts is advisable to ensure that the young couple are happy, healthy and* *long-lived. Is matching necessary when one contracts a second or even a third marriage ?*

Answer: Whether one marries for the first or the second or even the 3rd time, normally the objective is to be happy in the union. Therefore, when the first marriage has failed and a second marriage is contemplated, matching of charts continues to serve the same purpose of ensuring a reasonable degree of happiness and stability. Marriages are also contracted for money, prestige and other extraneous reasons but they do not fit into the concept of marriage as prevailing in India as a Vedic Samskara or Vedic sacrament. Matching of charts is meant to ensure a happy marriage and a life of contentment and satisfaction between the husband and the wife preparing them to pursue the objectives of *Grihasthasrama.*

Question: *What are the combinations for widowhood ?*

Answer: Many charts are deceptively misleading when it comes to identifying loss of spouse by death. Classical texts carry many combinations for such a tragedy. Some of these combinations work literally, others have to be suitably adapted.

Some combinations commonly found in almost all classical works for loss of husband (or wife) are :

(1)The lords of the 7th and 8th houses together and occupying the 8th house aspected by malefic planets.

(2) Rahu in the 7th, the 7th lord conjoining the Sun aspected by the 8th lord.

(3) Mars in the 8th with the 8th lord and Lagna in a malefic Navamsa.

(4) Rahu joined by Mars and Saturn in the 7th or 8th can show early widowhood.

(5) If the 7th lord is malefic and Mars and Saturn are in the 7th or the 8th.

(6) If the 7th and its lord are between malefics in conjunction with no benefics or not aspected by benefics.

(7) If the Navamsa lord of the 7th is in debility, eclipsed or combust or between evil planets and unfavorable Shadvargas.

(8) The Moon in Cancer in Saturn's Trimsamsa can also show widowhood.

(9) If Mars occupies the 7th, widowhood comes very soon after marriage.

The most commonly known combinations for widowhood are dominated by the position of Mars.

If Mars, bereft of the aspect or conjunction of an auspicious (or benefic) planet, is posited in the Ascendant, the 2nd, the 12th, the 4th, the 7th or the 8th, it indicates death of spouse.

But there is provision to overcome this Dosha in classical works according to which, if a man has a Yoga similar to the Yoga in a woman's chart for widowhood, then marriage between them leads to cancellation of such a Yoga. This is the principle behind balancing of malefic content or Dosha in charts for marriage.

(10) If malefics flank Venus on either side as in a

Papakartari Yoga or occupy the 4th, the 8th and the 12th from Venus jointly or severally, loss of spouse can occur by death.

(11) Likewise, the 7th lord in the 8th or the 8th lord in the 7th or a Parivartana or exchange of signs between the 7th and 8th lords can snatch away one's spouse.

(12) Yogas for widowhood gain strength if a Martian Navamsa is shown.

(13) If the Sun is in Lagna and Saturn in the 7th, loss of partner is shown.

(14) Venus, if conjoined with a malefic and with no benefic aspect, can cause death of spouse through fire.

(15) If Venus, caught between malefics, occupies the 8th or the 4th, loss of married partner is likely.

(16) If Venus and the Sun occupy the 5th, the 7th or the 9th, it shows loss of spouse.

(17) If Venus joined by Mars and Saturn is in the 7th house, loss of spouse is indicated.

(18) If Mars be in the 6th, Rahu in the 7th and Saturn in the 8th, loss of married partner is possible.

(19) If the Lagna lord is in debility or a debilitated planet occupies the Lagna, loss of spouse is the result.

(20) If Rahu and Saturn occupy the Lagna, the spouse may be lost due to scandals etc.

(21) If Venus be in the 6th, the 8th or the 12th in conjunction with either the 7th or the 2nd lord, loss of spouse is shown.

(22) Malefics in the 4th and the 8th from Venus indicate loss of spouse.

(23) If Venus be caught between malefics, one may lose one's spouse.

(24) If the 5th lord be in the 7th and the 7th lord be joined by a malefic, loss of spouse is indicated. In the case of a male chart, it can show death of wife through abortion or delivery.

(25) If Venus or the Moon occupy the 4th house in depression, loss of spouse is the result.

(26) If Venus be conjoined with the 6th lord, then also it shows loss of spouse.

In all these combinations, risking the charge of being repetitive, let me emphasise the influence by aspect or association of the Ascendant lord, sign-dispositor or Jupiter is of great help. No single combination should be taken in isolation to come to any conclusion.

Question: *What other factors can overcome Mars in the 7th ?*

Answer: There is a school of thought that holds Mars in the 7th is not harmful, if aspected by benefics — Jupiter, Venus or Mercury or if benefics occupy the 4th, 5th, 9th or 10th or even Lagna but themselves should not be in debility, combust or with the Nodes. In other words, Mars in the 7th can be curbed by a benefic in the Ascendant. primarily. This is just an application of Varahamihira's basic principle that Jupiter, Mercury or the Lagna lord in Lagna strengthen the Ascendant, and therefore, the horsocope in general. Likewise, malefics in Lagna can be deemed to aggravate the Dosha of Mars. But the best safeguard against Mars in the 7th is a similar placement of this planet in the other chart also.

***Question:* What significance does Vedha have ?**

Answer: Vedha is one of the more important Kuta factors in judging marital compatibility between two charts.

Vedha defines sets of asterisms that are mutually repellent. These sets are :

Aswini-Jyeshta, Bharani-Anuradha, Krittika-Visakha, Rohini-Swati, Aridra-Sravana, Punarvasu-Uttarashada, Pushya-Purvashada, Aslesha-Moola, Makha-Revati, Poorvaphalguni-Uttarabhadrapada, Uttaraphalguni-Poorvabhadrapada, Hasta-Satabhisha, and Mrigasira-Chitta, Dhanishta.

Aswini (0^0), Makha (120^0) and Moola (240^0) are known to be critical points of the Zodiac and are in mutual trine.

Taking Aswini and Jyeshta, the first pair, we find the two are equidistant from Makha. So also, the next pair Bharani and Anuradha are equidistant from the 120 point of the Zodiac or Makha. Krittika and Visakha, Rohini and Swati are also similarly situated. In other words, it implies if the Moons of the boy and the girl are situated in Nakshatras equidistant from Makha, there is bound to be unhappiness in their combined lives and so, Vedha is said to be present between the two.

Aridra and Sravana are equidistant from the 0^0 point or Aswini, Punarvasu and Uttarashada are also equidistant from this point, so also Pushya and Purvashada and Aslesha and Moola.

The pairs Makha-Revati, Poorvaphalguni-Uttarabhadrapada, Uttaraphalguni-Purvabhadrapada and Hasta-Sravana are equidistant from Moola. The forbidden pairs, therefore, follow a distinct astronomical pattern defined by each pair occupying the same distance from the Aswini, Makha and Moola triad.

Likewise, just as 0^0, 120^0 and 240^0 are deemed inauspicious or Gandanta parts of the Zodiac, their mid-points at 60^0, 180^0 and 300^0 of the Zodiac may also be deemed sensitive or critical points. These points correspond to the mid-points of the Nakshatras Mrigasira, Chitta and Dhanishta drawing mutually the taboo of Vedha.

In the example case of Jyeshta (male) and Anuradha (female) constellations, there is no Vedha or objection to the pair.

Question: *You say : "For a girl with Mars in the 8th, it is better the boy too has Mars in the 8th. But if the girl has Mars in the 7th, Mars in the 7th or 8th for the boy would be quite okay."*

I find this statement misleading and untenable due to the following reason :

The strength of Mangalya Bhava should be determined from the 8th house in the female horoscope. The 7th house indicates the husband and his prosperity, being the Kalatra Bhava.

In the male horoscope, the 7th house is the Kalatra Bhava and the 8th is the house of longevity. There is no Mangalya Bhava in a male horoscope.

In a female horoscope, malefics in the 7th and 8th houses indicate the death of the husband. Hence, the boy's horoscope to be matched with such girls, must have malefics of equal strength in the 7th house only.

For a girl with malefics in the 7th and a boy who has similar malefics in the 8th house is not a suitable match at all. Instead, it will speed up the death of the husband. What do you have to say ?

Ans: While the 8th house in a female chart is called Mangalya Bhava, the 8th house in a male chart is not referred to by that name only because of social reasons. But the 8th house of the boy has equally to do with the longevity or duration of the marital bond. Additionally, irrespective of whether it is a boy's or a girl's chart, the 8th house is the house of longevity also.

According to **Brihat Parasara Hora**, Chapter 80, Sloka 50, **स्त्रीणां वैधव्यदौ योगः पुंसां जन्मनि चेद् भवेत्** which means, the same combinations for widowhood in a woman's chart, if found in a man's chart show loss of wife. Therefore, Mars in the 8th which is a strong factor for *vydhavya* or loss of husband if present in a male chart can also be understood to show loss of wife in the latter case. Apart from the astrological factor, it is common knowledge that a woman losing her husband becomes more vulnerable than a man losing his wife. Therefore, it was always thought safe that the woman must be insured against such a contingency. Mars in the 7th may or may not destroy the marital bond as much as Mars in the 8th. That is, the Dosha of Mars in the 8th becomes stronger than the Dosha of Mars in the 7th. Therefore, a woman with Mars in the 8th has a stronger Dosha than a man with Mars in the 7th which makes her more vulnerable to loss of spouse than the man, astrologically speaking. In order to offset such a result, it is better to have Mars in the 8th in the male chart also for a girl with Mars in the 8th.

The following illustration is a good example.

Boy: Born 26-5-1961 at 10-00 p.m. (IST) at 13N, 77E 35 with a balance of 4 years, 1 month and 20 days of Mars Dasa at birth.

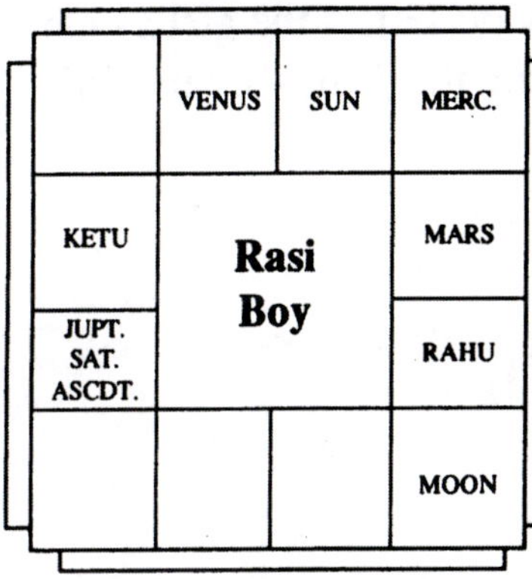

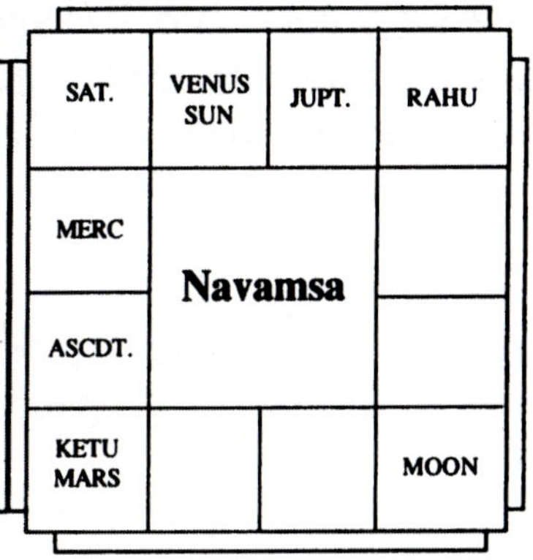

Girl: Born 18-7-1968 at 3-35 p.m. at 13 N, 77 E 35 with a balance of 17 years, 1 month and 15 days of Venus Dasa at birth.

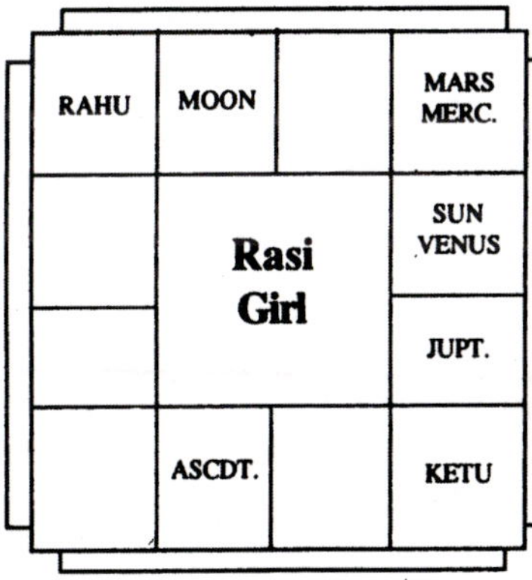

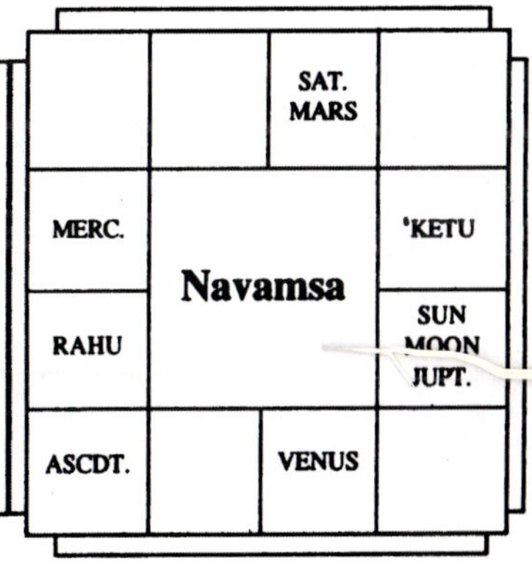

In this case, the boy's chart has Mars in the 7th. The girl has Mars in the 8th. The marriage did not survive for long and broke up in 1999 with a divorce. The girl's chart has Mars in the 8th which is weightier than Mars in the 7th in the boy's case. The charts appear to have been approved under the wrong notion, the malefic in the 7th in the boy's chart was enough to balance the 8th house Mars in the girl's chart.

As a general rule, it is always better the girl's chart has slightly less Dosha than the boy's even while evaluating Dosha Samya. ●